Yellowstone National Park

Yellowstone National Park: the Basics

History and Facts

Established: March 1, 1872

Visitors: 3,500,000

Designations: the world's first national park; World Heritage Site; Biosphere Reserve

Natural Historic Landmarks: 25 sites including museums at Fishing Bridge, Madison, and Norris Trailside; Northeast Entrance Station, Obsidian Cliff, Old Faithful Inn, Fort Yellowstone District

National Register of Historic Places: including Mammoth Hot Springs District, Old Faithful Area District, Roosevelt Lodge District, Lake Hotel, Lamar Buffalo Ranch

National Scenic Trail: Continental Divide National Scenic Trail

States: 96% in Wyoming, 3% in Montana, 1% in Idaho

Time zone: Mountain Standard Time (MST)

Official Park Website: nps.gov/yell

Physical Features

Acreage: approximately 2,221,766 acres

Elevation: lowest point: 5,282' at Reese Creek; highest point: 11,358' at Eagle Peak

Geologic features: an active volcano; about 1,000–3,000 earthquakes annually; over 10,000 hydrothermal features, including over 300 geysers; the largest concentration of active geysers in the world, representing about half of the world's total; one of world's largest calderas measuring 45 by 30 miles; petrified trees

Water resources: about 150 lakes; 14 rivers; over 160 creeks; over 290 waterfalls

Annual precipitation: avg. 15.4"; ranges from 10" at the northern boundary to 80" in the southwest corner; avg. total snowfall 72.1"

Temperature range (F): 99°F to −66°F; average temperature at Mammoth: 9°F in January, 80°F in July

Plant species: approximately 1,150 native flowering species; about 200 invasive plants; 186 lichens; over 406 thermophiles

Animal species: 332 birds; 67 mammals; 16 fish; 6 reptiles; 5 amphibians, 116 butterflies

Wildlife population estimates: 3,900 bison; 10,000–20,000 elk, 1,000–1,300 mule deer, 450 bighorn sheep; 200–351 pronghorn; 200–300 mountain goats; less than 200 white-tailed deer; 95 wolves; less than 200 moose; 14–23 cougars; 150 grizzlies; black bears are "common"

Facilities

Entrance stations: 5: North Entrance near Gardiner, MT (open all year); West Entrance near West Yellowstone, MT (mid-April to early November); East Entrance about 1 hour from Cody, WY (mid-April to early November); South Entrance connects with Grand Teton National Park via John D. Rockefeller Jr. Memorial Parkway, closest town is Jackson, WY (mid-May to early November); Northeast Entrance near Silver Gate and Cooke City, MT (open year-round for vehicle access through Gardiner, MT); US 212 east of Cooke City is closed to wheeled vehicles mid-October through late May.) All dates are subject to change.

Visitor centers/museums/contact stations: 9+: Albright Visitor Center; Canyon Visitor Education Center; Fishing Bridge Visitor Center; Grant Visitor Center; Madison Information Station and Junior Ranger Station; Museum of the National Park Ranger; Norris Geyser Basin Museum & Information Station; Old Faithful Visitor Education Center; West Thumb Information Center; and West Yellowstone Visitor Information Center NPS Desk located in West Yellowstone Montana Chamber of Commerce

Roads: 310 miles paved roads; 156 miles unpaved roads

Trails: approximately 1,000 miles of trails; 92 trailheads

Boardwalks: over 15 miles

Campgrounds: 301 backcountry sites; 7 NPS-operated with 450 sites; 5 concession-operated with 1,700 sites

Picnic areas: 52

Marina: Bridge Bay

Lodging: 9 lodges (2,000+ rooms): Mammoth Hot Springs Hotel and Cabins, Roosevelt Lodge Cabins, Canyon Lodge and Cabins, Lake Lodge Cabins, Lake Hotel and Cabins, Grant Village, Old Faithful Inn, Old Faithful Lodge Cabins, Snow Lodge and Cabins

Food: numerous restaurants, cafeterias, light meals, and snacks: Canyon Lodge, Grant Village, Mammoth Hot Springs, Lake Village, Old Faithful, Roosevelt, Fishing Bridge, Bridge Bay, Tower Fall

Fuel: spring through fall: Canyon, Fishing Bridge, Grant Village, Mammoth, Old Faithful, Tower Junction; winter snowmobile fuel: Canyon, Fishing Bridge, Mammoth, Grant Village, Old Faithful

Medical Services: 3 clinics: Mammoth, Lake Village, Old Faithful

Nature Guide to Yellowstone National Park

Ann and Rob Simpson

GUILFORD, CONNECTICUT
HELENA, MONTANA

FALCONGUIDES®

An imprint of Rowman & Littlefield
Falcon, FalconGuides, and Outfit Your Mind are registered trademarks of
Rowman & Littlefield.

Distributed by NATIONAL BOOK NETWORK

British Library Cataloguing-in-Publication Information available

Library of Congress Cataloging-in-Publication data is available on file.

ISBN 978-1-4930-0967-1 (paperback)
ISBN 978-1-4930-1481-1 (e-book)

∞™ The paper used in this publication meets the minimum
requirements of American National Standard for Information Sciences—
Permanence of Paper for Printed Library Materials, ANSI/NISO
Z39.48-1992.

Contents

YELLOWSTONE NATIONAL PARK

To Livingston

GALLATIN NATIONAL FOREST

GALLATIN NATIONAL FOREST

Shitwater River

Stillwater River

Beartooth Highway closed from mid-October to late May

212

Cooke City

Silver Gate

Northeast Entrance

ABSAROKA

RANGE

SHOSHONE NATIONAL FOREST

Pollux Peak

Saddle Mountain

Miller Creek

Cache Creek

The Thunderer

Pyramid Peak

Barronette Peak 10404 ft 3171 m

Yellowstone Association Institute

Pebble Creek

Lamar River

Trout Lake

Soda Butte Creek

Slough Creek

LAMAR VALLEY

Lamar River

MIRROR PLATEAU

BUFFALO PLATEAU

Buffalo Creek

Hellroaring Creek

Slough Creek

Buffalo Fork

Slough Creek

Park road between the North Entrance and Cooke City is open all year

MONTANA
WYOMING

SPECIMEN RIDGE

Pelican Cone

Hellroaring Mountain

Yellowstone River

Tower Junction

Tower Fall

Tower-Roosevelt

GRAND CANYON OF THE YELLOWSTONE

White Lake

Pelican Creek

Phantom Lake

Petrified Tree

Calcite Springs Overlook

Mount Washburn

Dunraven Pass

Inspiration Point

Artist Point

Lower Falls

Upper Falls

Lehardy Rapids

Sulphur Caldron

Mud Volcano
Nez Perce Ford

Yellowstone River

Blacktail Plateau Drive

BLACKTAIL DEER PLATEAU

Wraith Falls

Blacktail Ponds

Undine Falls

Mount Everts

Jardine

Gardiner

North Entrance

Mammoth Hot Springs

Visitor Center
Park Headquarters
Mammoth Hot Springs Terraces
Road closed from early November to late April

Observation Peak

Canyon Village
Visitor Education Center

HAYDEN VALLEY

PLATEAU

89

To Livingston

Swan Lake

Bunsen Peak

Sheepeater Cliff

Indian Creek

Mount Holmes

GALLATIN RANGE

Grizzly Lake

Twin Lakes

Obsidian Cliff

Roaring Mountain

Norris Geyser Basin Museum

Lava Creek

Tower Creek

Cascade Creek

Virginia Cascade

Norris Junction

Norris

Artist Paint Pots

Gibbon River

Steamboat Geyser

Monument Geyser Basin

Information Station, Museum and Bookstore

Madison

Road closed from early November to late April

West Yellowstone Visitor Information Center

West Entrance

Mt Haynes

MADISON VALLEY

Madison River

Firehole River

Gibbon Falls

Madison Junction

Information Station Bookstore

Firehole Falls

WYOMING
MONTANA

191

287

191
287

20

West Yellowstone

To Ashton

To Quake Lake

Gallatin River

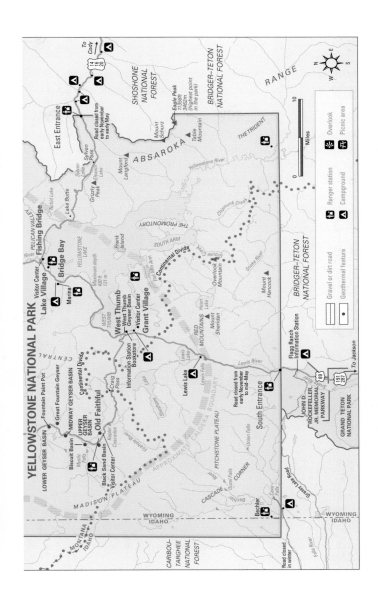

Acknowledgments

Many thanks to the superb park personnel and volunteers of Yellowstone National Park, who have dedicated their lives to preserving the natural resources of the park and sharing the natural wonders of the park with visitors. We would especially like to thank Dan and Cindy Hartman for sharing their wealth of knowledge about the park's natural history. Others who have given insight or helped contribute in other ways to this book are Heidi Anderson, Tami Blackford, Rick McIntyre, Bonnie Quinn, Carol McClure, John Harmer, Brad Bulin, Shauna Baron, George Bumann, Doug Smith, Moe Cairns, Sue Consolo-Murphy, Mark Haroldson, and all of the volunteers and instructors for the Yellowstone Association Institute. Our thanks also to Debbie Collins, Ken Voorhis,

Cowbirds keep company with a bison.

A quiet lake accented with arrowleaf balsamroot.

and the staff and members of the Yellowstone Association for their continued support of the interpretive and educational mission of the park. We would also like to thank all the staff at Falcon-Guides and Rowman & Littlefield, whose support and efforts made this Nature Guide to the National Parks series a reality. We would like to dedicate this book to our family, who has supported us with encouragement and understanding during the research, writing, and photography of this nature guide.

To the reader, we hope that this guide helps to open your eyes to the wonders of nature and, in doing so, will generate a spark of love for the plants and animals that rely on us for their continued existence in important natural habitats such as those in Yellowstone National Park.

About Yellowstone Association

The Yellowstone Association (YA), in partnership with the National Park Service, connects people to Yellowstone National Park and our natural world through education. Founded in 1933, the Yellowstone Association is a nonprofit educational organization that has provided over $59 million in aid to Yellowstone National Park since its inception. The Association is the National Park Service's primary partner in providing educational programs, exhibits, and publications for park visitors.

Operations include twelve educational park stores with gross sales of $3.7 million; the YA Institute, which offers more than 600 in-depth courses each year; and a membership program with nearly 35,000 members. Revenues from sales and memberships allow YA to make an annual cash donation to the National Park Service for education and research in Yellowstone. Eighty-nine cents of every dollar spent goes directly to YA's educational mission. To learn more, please visit YellowstoneAssociation.org or call (406) 848-2400.

The Yellowstone Association supports educational efforts in the park.

About Yellowstone Association Institute

The Yellowstone Association Institute has helped connect thousands of people to Yellowstone with their in-depth educational programs. The Institute was founded in 1976 and offers 600 courses each year on the park's plants, wildlife, geology, and history. Programs are offered year-round and combine just the right amount of education and recreation. The Institute offers four program types: private tours, lodging and learning programs, field seminars, and youth and college programs. Institute educational programs are based at the Lamar Buffalo Ranch, Yellowstone Overlook Field Campus, at park hotels, and in the backcountry.

Exciting natural history and wildlife learning adventures are offered through the Yellowstone Association Institute.

The stark beauty of Yellowstone allows visitors solitude and time for reflection.

Introduction

The *Nature Guide to Yellowstone National Park* is an easy-to-use, pocket-size field guide to help visitors identify some of the most common plants, animals, and natural features of the park. Technical terms have been kept to a minimum, and color pictures accompany the descriptions. Perfectly sized to fit easily into a daypack, this compact field guide is filled with interesting information about each organism, including natural history and ethnobotanical notes and other historical remarks. We care for the things that we know. Intended as an introduction to nature in the Yellowstone National Park, this small book will hopefully spark an interest in the natural world and generate further interest in caring for and supporting the environment. You can refer to the "References" section at the end of this book for more information and resources for in-depth identification purposes.

About Yellowstone National Park

A land of earthquakes, bubbling mud pots, hot springs, and fumaroles, Yellowstone National Park is celebrated worldwide for its impressive geysers, including the iconic Old Faithful. As well as its famous thermal features, Yellowstone is home to the most abundant assemblages of wild animals in the United States. Observable dramatic life-and-death encounters in the wild have prompted Yellowstone to be dubbed the "Serengeti of North America." Yellowstone's diverse wildlife inhabitants include bison, elk, bighorn sheep, bear, moose, coyotes, and wolves that survive in this protected park. The ultimate national park, Yellowstone's natural features are so incredibly unique that in 1872, President Ulysses S. Grant signed the papers to establish Yellowstone as the first national park in the world, forever protecting the abundant wildlife and geothermal features. Over three million annual visitors to Yellowstone quickly observe that the grassy valleys, swiftly flowing rivers, and soaring flower-laden mountains provide food and

Roaming free once more, the wolves of Yellowstone have returned as one of the top predators.

habitat for an abundance of wild plants and animals. This easy-to-use field guide will help visitors identify over 200 species of mammals, birds, butterflies, insects, fish, wildflowers, mushrooms, and more in Yellowstone.

Located mainly in the northwest corner of Wyoming, the park's boundaries also include a portion of both Montana and Idaho. This huge park, encompassing over 2 million acres, includes vast forests, mountains, and grasslands, as well as Yellowstone Lake, which is the largest high-altitude lake in North America. Yellowstone lies at the heart of the Greater Yellowstone Ecosystem, protecting the last remaining nearly intact ecosystem in the northern temperate zone. With soaring mountain peaks, sagebrush-studded prairies, plunging waterfalls, deep canyons, and a vast array of native charismatic mammals, Yellowstone was named an UNESCO World Heritage Site and a Biosphere Reserve.

A park of significant diversity and magnificence, Yellowstone protects a wide array of plants and animals, including herds of wild bison that once roamed the grasslands in huge numbers. Some plants including the Yellowstone sand verbena have their entire range within park boundaries. It is highly recommended that you begin your visit with a stop at one of the visitor centers, where you can pick up a park map and learn about activities such as the Junior Ranger program and other events. The park offers ranger-led programs that help educate visitors about the many wonders of Yellowstone. In Canyon Village, the Canyon Visitor Education Center is a great place to learn about the natural volcanic and glacial processes that shaped the park.

There is an entrance fee for Yellowstone National Park; see the park website for current costs at nps.gov/yell. The entrance fee includes a seven-day entrance permit for the park. Annual or Lifetime Passes are possible alternatives to the seven-day entrance fee. Good for one year, the America the Beautiful Interagency Annual Pass provides entrance to most federal recreation sites across the country. Also available is the lifetime Interagency Senior Pass for US citizens age sixty-two or older. Permanently disabled citizens are eligible for a free Access Pass; active duty military members and dependents are eligible for a free Annual Pass.

Although the park is open daily, most visitor services close from early November to mid-April.

Seasonal activities, lodging, camping, and other information are offered in the Yellowstone National Park Trip Planner and the official park newspaper, available online at nps.gov/yell. During the peak visitor seasons (June through August), the lodges and campgrounds fill early, and advance planning is necessary. Lodging and camping reservations are available at yellowstonenationalpark lodges.com, or (307) 344-7311 or (866) 439-7375. Food, lodging, fuel, and other services are also available at the local towns bordering the park; see "Gateway Towns." Outdoor classes, programs,

The age-old struggle for life and death continues in the wilds of Yellowstone.

and workshops highlighting nature and cultural studies from birds to wildflowers to geology are offered throughout the year by the Yellowstone Association Institute. Please consider joining the association's efforts to support the education and research projects in the park: (406) 848-2400, yellowstoneassociation.org.

Common Destinations in or near Yellowstone National Park

Most visitor services in Yellowstone National Park are open mid-April through early November. Camping reservations for five campgrounds in the park (including Madison, Fishing Bridge RV Park, Bridge Bay, Canyon, and Grant Village) may be reserved at yellowstonenationalparklodges.com, (307) 344-7311, or (866) 439-7375, or for same-day reservations, (307) 344-7901. Seven campgrounds including Mammoth, Norris, Tower Fall, Indian Creek, Pebble Creek, Slough Creek, and Lewis Lake all are on a first-come, first-served basis. Fuel and other services can be found in towns at the entrances to the park. Restrooms are located at visitor centers, major attractions, and at most picnic areas. Roads in the park are normally open twenty-four hours a day during the warm seasons, but severe weather, fire, or other emergencies may necessitate closure at any time. The only road open to personal vehicles in the winter is the North Entrance road at Gardiner, Montana, to Mammoth Hot Springs and Cooke City, Montana, but no farther. For more current road information, call (307) 344-2117 or see the Yellowstone National Park website at nps.gov/yell/planyourvisit/hours.htm. (**Note:** Cell phones do not work in many areas of the park.)

Services in Yellowstone

Gas Stations (24-hour self-serve fuel); (406) 848-7548 for assistance
    Canyon: repairs and towing
    Fishing Bridge: repairs and towing
    Grant Village: repairs and towing
    Mammoth Hot Springs
    Old Faithful: repairs and towing

Tower Junction

Snowmobile fuel: Canyon Village, Fishing Bridge, Mammoth, Grant Village, Old Faithful

Lodging—Reservations: (866) 439-7375 or yellowstonenational parklodges.com/lodging/reservations

Canyon Lodge & Cabins: near the Grand Canyon of the Yellowstone

Grant Village: southwestern shore of Yellowstone Lake

Lake Hotel: north shore of Yellowstone Lake

Lake Lodge: north shore of Yellowstone Lake

Mammoth Hot Springs Hotel & Cabins: near North Entrance (also open in winter)

Old Faithful Inn: near Old Faithful geyser in southwest part of park

Old Faithful Lodge Cabins: near Old Faithful geyser in southwest part of park

Old Faithful Snow Lodge & Cabins: near Old Faithful geyser in southwest part of park (also open in winter; transportation via snowcoach or snow mobile)

Roosevelt Lodge & Cabins: near Tower Fall on the park's northern range

Camping—**Campground Reservations:** (307) 344-7311, (866) 439-7375, same-day reservations (307) 344-7901; yellowstone nationalparklodges.com

Madison: 278 sites (no utility hookups)

Fishing Bridge RV Park: 346 sites (hard-sided units only; maximum length 40 feet) (pay shower, coin laundry nearby)

Bridge Bay: 432 sites (no utility hookups; pay shower, coin laundry nearby)

Canyon: 273 sites (no utility hookups; pay shower, coin laundry nearby)

Grant Village: 430 sites (pay shower and coin laundry nearby)

Mammoth: 85 sites (first come, first served; pay shower)

Norris: 100+ sites (first come, first served)

Tower Fall: 31 sites (first come, first served; pay shower 2 miles away at Roosevelt Lodge)

Indian Creek: 75 sites (first come, first served)

Pebble Creek: 27 sites (first come, first served)

Slough Creek: 23 sites (first come, first served)

Lewis Lake: 85 sites (first come, first served)

Visitor Centers / Information plus Books & Field Guides

Albright Visitor Center: Mammoth Hot Springs, (307) 344-2263

Canyon Visitor Education Center: Canyon Village, (307) 344-2550

Fishing Bridge Museum and Visitor Center: Fishing Bridge, (307) 344-2450

Grant Visitor Center: Grant Village, (307) 344-2650

Madison Information Station & Junior Ranger Station: Madison Junction, (307) 344-2821

Museum of the National Park Ranger: 1 mile north of Norris Geyser Basin, (307) 344-7353

Norris Geyser Basin Museum & Information Station: Norris Geyser Basin, (307) 344-2812

Old Faithful Visitor Education Center: Old Faithful, (307) 344-2751

West Thumb Information Center: West Thumb, (307) 344-2650

West Yellowstone Visitor Information Center, NPS Desk: located outside the park in West Yellowstone Chamber of Commerce, (307) 344-2876

Marina, Boat Tours & Trail Rides

Canyon: trail rides

Mammoth: trail rides

Roosevelt: trail rides, stagecoach rides

Bridge Bay: marina, boat tours

Restaurants, Cafeterias & Snack Shops

Canyon Village: Canyon Lodge Dining Room, Canyon Lodge cafeteria, general store, Canyon Adventures outdoor store, Lodge Picnic Shop

Grant Village: Grant Village dining room, Grant Village Lake House Restaurant, general store, mini store

Yellowstone Lake: Lake Yellowstone Hotel Dining Room, Lake Lodge Cafeteria, hotel deli, general store

Mammoth Hot Springs: Mammoth Hot Springs Hotel Dining Room, Terrace Grill, general store

Old Faithful: Old Faithful Inn Dining Room, Old Faithful Lodge Cafeteria, Old Faithful Basin Store

Old Faithful Snow Lodge: Old Faithful Snow Lodge Restaurant, Geyser Grill

Tower-Roosevelt: Roosevelt Lodge Dining Room, Tower Fall Store

Groceries, Supplies & Gifts

Canyon Village: general store, groceries, gear, camp supplies

Fishing Bridge: general store, groceries, camp supplies

Grant Village: general store, groceries, gear, camp supplies

Lake Village: general store

Mammoth Hot Springs: general store, gear

Old Faithful: general store, gear

Tower: general store

Roosevelt Lodge and Cabins: mini store

Showers & Laundry

Canyon Campground: showers, laundry

Fishing Bridge RV Park: showers, laundry

Grant Village Campground: showers, laundry

Lake Lodge: laundry

Mammoth Hotel: showers

Old Faithful Inn: showers

Snow Lodge: laundry

Roosevelt Lodge and Cabins: showers

Bridge Bay: mini store

Medical Clinic

 Mammoth Hot Springs: year-round except weekends and
  holidays, (307) 344-7965
 Old Faithful: (307) 545-7325
 Lake Village, Bridge Bay: (307) 242-7241

Post Office (hours vary)

 Mammoth Hot Springs: open year-round, closed Saturday,
  Sunday, and holidays
 Old Faithful
 Grant Village
 Lake Village
 Canyon Village

Yellowstone Association

Yellowstone Association Headquarters and Visitor Center: information, field guides, trail guides, reference books, gear, gifts. Mem-
berships available here. Primary nonprofit partner in providing
education in Yellowstone. Proceeds benefit park. 308 Park St., Gardiner, MT 59030; (406) 848-2400; yellowstoneassociation.org.

 Yellowstone Association Institute: programs, workshops,
classes. (406) 848-2400; yellowstoneassociation.org/experience.
If you have questions about Yellowstone Association Institute or
need more details on any of our programs, contact us directly at:
 registrar@yellowstoneassociation.org or (406) 848-2400

Yellowstone Park Foundation

Nonprofit official fund-raising partner of Yellowstone National
Park. 222 E. Main St., Ste. 301, Bozeman, MT 59715; (406) 586-
6303; ypf.org.

Gateway Towns
West Entrance

West Yellowstone, Montana: lodging, food, fuel. West Yellowstone
Chamber of Commerce, 30 Yellowstone Ave., West Yellowstone,
MT 59758; (406) 646-7701; destinationyellowstone.com.

North Entrance

Gardiner, Montana: lodging, food, fuel. Gardiner Chamber of Commerce, 222 Park St., Gardiner, MT 59030; (406) 848-7971; gardinerchamber.com.

Northeast Entrance

Silver Gate and Cooke City, Montana: lodging, food, fuel. Visitor's Center, 206 W. Main St., Cooke City, MT 59020; (406) 838-2495; cookecity chamber.org.

In winter, the only road open to wheeled vehicles in the park is from the North Entrance at Gardiner to the Northeast Entrance.

Park conservation is encouraged through the Junior Ranger program.

In winter, roads east of Cooke City are closed.

East Entrance

Limited services at East Entrance.

Cody, Wyoming: lodging, food, fuel. Cody Chamber of Commerce, 836 Sheridan Ave., Cody, WY 82414; (307) 587-2777; codychamber.org.

South Entrance

Limited services at South Entrance.

John D. Rockefeller Jr. Memorial Highway (7.3 miles) leads to the north entrance of Grand Teton National Park, (307) 739-3300; nps.gov/grte.

Jackson, Wyoming: lodging, food, fuel. Jackson Hole Chamber of Commerce, 112 Center St., Jackson, WY 83001; (307) 733-3316; jacksonholechamber.com.

Driving Times

In a park as large and mountainous as Yellowstone, many people underestimate how long it takes to drive to destinations within and outside the park. Within the park, there are also unexpected delays due to traffics jams at wildlife sightings, bison or other wild animals that block the road, road construction, detours, and so on; therefore, driving times vary greatly. A good rule of thumb is to double the mileage to estimate your driving time (e.g., if your destination is 30 miles away, estimate that it will take approximately 60 minutes of driving time). Remember that the fastest speed in the park is 45 miles an hour (mph), and it is often slower in certain areas. The park roads were designed in a rough figure-eight pattern, with major destinations at junctions. Starting from the northwest corner, the major destinations are Mammoth Hot Springs, Tower-Roosevelt, Canyon Village, Fishing Bridge / Lake Village, and Bridge Bay. West Thumb and Grant Village are the southernmost destinations. Continuing south to north, next is Old Faithful, Madison, then Norris, which brings you back to Mammoth Hot Springs. For current road conditions in the park, call (307) 344-2117 or visit nps.gov/yell. For the safety of wildlife and humans, please obey the park speed limits.

Carpets of colorful wildflowers, including bright arrowleaf balsamroot, create stunning wild meadow gardens.

Driving Times (Approximate)

Starting Point	Destination	Miles	Time
North Entrance at Gardiner, MT	Mammoth	5	15 min
	Livingston, MT	55	1 hr
	Bozeman, MT	84	1 hr, 45min
Mammoth	Tower-Roosevelt	18	45 min
	Norris	21	1 hr
Tower-Roosevelt	Northeast Entrance at Silver Gate / Cooke City	29	1 hr
	Canyon Village	19	1 hr
Northeast Entrance at Silver Gate / Cooke City	Red Lodge, MT	70	1 hr, 45 min
	Billings, MT	135	2 hr, 45 min
Canyon	Lake Area	16	45 min
	Norris	12	30 min
Fishing Bridge	East Entrance	27	1 hr
East Entrance	Cody, WY	53	1 hr
Lake Area	West Thumb / Grant	21	45 min
West Thumb / Grant	South Entrance	22	45 min
South Entrance	Grand Teton National Park (via John D. Rockefeller Jr. Memorial Highway)	7	15 min
	Jackson, WY	58	1 hr, 30 min
Old Faithful	West Entrance	30	1 hr
	South Entrance	39	1 hr, 20 min
	North Entrance	56	1 hr, 45 min
	Northeast Entrance	90–100	2 hr, 30 min–3 hr
	East Entrance	65	2 hr
Madison	Norris	14	30 min
West Entrance at West Yellowstone, MT	Idaho Falls, ID	107	2 hr

Stunning scenery at the Grand Canyon of the Yellowstone awaits the 3.5 million visitors to Yellowstone each year.

Safety Notes

The maximum speed limit is generally 45 mph, but in some areas it drops to 25 mph or less. There are some steep grades and many winding curves, some with very small sight distances. Use caution when you are passing by or pulling out of one of the overlooks along the road. Always use pullouts to view wildlife. Allow time to pull over and enjoy the wildlife and scenery, and be aware that others may be distracted by looking at the view and not at the road. Be aware that wildlife such as bison, bear, coyote, and elk may dash onto the road with little notice. When it is snowy or icy, avoid driving if possible.

Geothermal formations create unusual dangers in Yellowstone. You must stay on boardwalks and designated trails. In many places, the crust is thin, and scalding water lies just inches away. Keep children with you and never let them run ahead of you. Pets are prohibited in thermal areas. Toxic gases may exist at dangerous levels in some hydrothermal areas. If you feel sick, leave immediately.

Always let someone know when you go for a hike. Dress in layers, as weather conditions can change rapidly. Snow can occur at any time of year. Be aware of fast-moving streams and waterfalls. Dehydration and sunburn can be prevented by drinking plenty of water and applying sunscreen. Do not drink untreated water from springs or streams as the seemingly clean water may harbor parasites, including *Giardia lamblia*, which causes severe diarrhea.

What we experience in nature inspires wonder and amazement.

About 300 species of birds can be found in Yellowstone including gorgeous lazuli buntings.

Never feed wildlife. Not only is it illegal, but it endangers the welfare of the animal. Stay a safe distance from all wildlife. Stay at least 100 yards away from bears and wolves. Also stay at least 25 yards away from all other large animals, including bison, elk, bighorn sheep, deer, moose, and coyotes. Major predators, including grizzly bears, black bears, and mountain lions, live in the park. When hiking, always carry bear spray and know how to use it. Most bears will avoid you if they hear you coming. If you encounter a bear, make your presence known by talking quietly and slowly back away. If the bear approaches you, make noises such as yelling and clapping your hands. Avoid hiking alone, and never let small children run ahead of you on trails. Keep them beside you, and pick them up if

Viewing wildlife in action, visitors to Yellowstone experience nature at its essence.

14

a bear is encountered. Obey area closures, as some are closed due to large bear populations. Proper food storage is required in Yellowstone. If you have a surprise encounter with a bear, do not run, but slowly back away.

Please report emergencies, such as accidents, uncontrolled fires, or other safety hazards, by calling 911. Removal or damage of any natural or archaeological objects is prohibited. We do not recommend the use or consumption of any plants or fungi as they could be poisonous or otherwise harmful.

Conservation Note

Please leave wildflowers and other plants where they grow. When hiking, stay on established trails and watch

Please take only pictures, as even the tiny chipmunks depend on the wildflowers for food.

The world's first national park, Yellowstone greets visitors from around the globe.

where you put your feet to avoid damaging plants. Especially in cliff areas, avoid trampling plants and lichens, as some of them may only be able to exist in these special conditions. Please keep in mind that it is illegal to pick, dig, or damage any plant. Please report any suspicious activity, such as plant poaching, to a park ranger. Remember that all natural resources are protected in the park, including the rocks, minerals, and pinecones. Please leave them for others to observe and enjoy.

How to Use This Guide

Common and Scientific Name

In an effort to create consistent communication worldwide, each organism has a Latin name, consisting of genus and species, that is unique to that organism. Common names of families are given with the scientific family name in parentheses. In many cases, an organism may have many common names, often depending on locality. In addition, genetic research is rapidly discovering new inherent relationships and associations, therefore the taxonomic status of many organisms may change with the new information. In general, organisms are listed taxonomically by order, family, and then genus. And some are listed alphabetically within their category.

Photo Tips

With abundant wildlife and spectacular scenery at every turn, Yellowstone's magnificence inspires the photographer in each of us. A few must-shoot images in Yellowstone include Old Faithful, herds of free-roaming bison and pronghorn in Lamar Valley, the Grand Canyon of the Yellowstone, Yellowstone Lake at sunset, Grand Prismatic Spring, Mammoth Hot Springs terraces, and the gorgeous wildflower display and scenics on Mount Washburn.

The incredible viewing access to large animals in the wild attracts wildlife photographers from around the world. Even though wildlife is easily seen, the animals are typically at a distance, and therefore you generally need to use a telephoto lens to zoom in on wildlife and keep the eye in focus. Never approach wildlife too closely just to get a picture. If your behavior changes the behavior of the animal, you are too close. For scenics, a tripod is necessary, especially for low-light conditions in the early morning or evening. Sharp focus is the key to taking great nature photos. Overcast days offer nice soft lighting for wildflowers and animals. In deep shade, increase the ISO or use a flash. Bright, sunny days create harsh shadows, and a flash will add detail to the dark shaded areas of the flower. Image-stabilization capability will help stop camera motion. For more advanced camera systems, shooting close-ups at f16 with a flash will give more depth of field and stop motion. When taking wildflower photos, be careful not to trample other plants.

Tips for Wildlife Viewing in Yellowstone

Being in the right place at the right time to see wildlife is often a matter of luck. However, you can stack the odds in your favor if you follow these wildlife viewing tips.

Protected within the boundaries of Yellowstone, sometimes wildlife becomes the spectator.

Timing. Animals are most active in the morning and evening. Often by late morning, the animals move into the cool forest and only come back out in the evening. In winter, the animals are more visible, and this is a great time to visit Yellowstone. Spring is the time to see baby animals, so plan your visit for April through June if you want to see wild babies.

Define your goal. If you want to see wolves or bears, you need to go to their typical habitat. Of course, spotting wildlife is hit or miss, but you can increase your chances of seeing a particular species if you figure out when and where it is most likely to be found. Helpful hints about where you might find the various species are included in many of the descriptions in this guide.

Ask a ranger. A stop at a visitor center can prove invaluable, as the rangers are very helpful with advice about where your best chances of seeing a particular species may be.

Location. Do your best to be at a location in the park where your target species has been seen. With so many wildlife watchers in the park, when someone spots an animal, crowds often gather quickly. Watch for these "wildlife jams," but be very cautious about pulling your car completely off the road into a designated parking area. Also be cautious about stepping out of your car into traffic, and keep a close eye on children who might dart out into the road. Remain in your vehicle if an animal approaches. Many animals, such as wolves and grizzlies, are attracted to carcasses, so keep your eyes open when you find one.

Have the right equipment. Before your trip to Yellowstone, consider purchasing a good pair of binoculars (or several for each member of your party), as you will be sorry if you have to hand your binoculars to someone else just as the action is occurring. Although some of the animals, such as bison, may walk directly in front of your car, you will see most at a distance, and a good pair of binoculars can bring them in so you can enjoy watching their behavior. Binoculars with image stabilization take the shake out of holding them by hand and allow you to see clearly from a distance. If you have been bitten by the wildlife-watching bug and just can't get enough, you may consider purchasing a spotting scope for super-close views. (Spotting scopes are small telescopes designed for viewing wildlife.) You will also need to purchase a tripod for your spotting scope. If possible, get one that is not silver, as light can reflect off the legs and startle animals. As with all optics, the lens quality varies greatly. Because equipment is often kept and enjoyed for a lifetime, try to get the best quality you can afford.

Practice safe and respectful wildlife watching. Safety is paramount when wildlife watching. No matter how large or small, these animals are truly wild, and many visitors are injured by not following safe practices. Do not get too close to an animal just to take a photo. Carry bear spray when hiking and do not hike alone. More injuries are caused by bison than any other animal in the park; do not underestimate their power. Bison are unpredictable and dangerous and can easily outrun a human; every year visitors are injured by bison, including life-threatening gorings. Respect wild animals and keep your distance. It is illegal to harass any animal in the park.

Yellowstone's iconic geysers provide stunning photographic opportunities.

Suggested Nature Hikes and Wildlife Viewing Areas

The following areas or trails are suggested for the general public and families who want to see wildlife, wildflowers, and other natural features of Yellowstone National Park. Some of the recommended trails are wheelchair accessible or accessible with assistance. Of course, the wild animals and plants of the park may not always be where expected, so it is a good idea to first stop at a visitor center and check with a park ranger about recent sightings. To find other attractive hikes, consult a topographic map or hiking guides such as *Best Easy Day Hikes: Yellowstone National Park* and *Hiking Yellowstone National Park* (FalconGuides). These and other interpretive publications are offered in the visitor centers in the park. Also, see the park website for some printable maps of certain popular areas in the park (nps.gov/yell/planyourvisit/index.htm).

One of the best ways to learn about wildlife, nature, and other park features from experts in their fields is to sign up for a class or field seminar with the nonprofit Yellowstone Association Institute (yellowstoneassociation.org). Always maintain a safe distance and never feed wildlife. Please do not pick any wildflowers or remove any natural objects from the park. Remember, you are more likely to see wild animals during the early morning and evening when they are more active. For their safety and yours, pets are not allowed on trails, even in the backcountry, nor are they allowed on boardwalks such as those that surround Old Faithful; you can check with a park ranger for pet regulations or see the park website (nps.gov/yell/planyourvisit/pets.htm).

1. **Lamar Valley** (northern section between Tower Junction and Northeast Entrance). A wildlife extravaganza, the Lamar Valley holds the honor as one of the most wildlife-rich areas in the United States. Here large herds of bison range freely on the valley grasslands, joined by quiet pronghorn that remain alert to the ever-present danger of predators such as

wolves and grizzlies. At the confluence of the Lamar River and Soda Butte Creek, you can often spot playful otters frolicking in the fast running water, while American dippers plunge underwater. In winter, look for common goldeneye and mallards.

   a. **Trout Lake.** Yellowstone cutthroat spawn in June; also find grizzlies, otters, Barrow's goldeneye, eared grebe, dragonflies, Engelmann spruce, yarrow, fireweed, goldenrod, and puffball mushrooms.

   b. **Slough Creek.** This area is rich with wolves, bison, coyote, ground squirrels, golden eagle, three-toed woodpecker, mountain bluebird, sandhill crane, coot, cinnamon teal, green-winged teal, and butterflies.

   c. **Barronette Peak.** Bring your binoculars and spotting scope to the small parking lot along the road at Barronette Peak, as this is one of the best places in the park to spot nimble mountain goats as they take daredevil leaps from steep cliff edges. Wildflowers fill the meadow adjacent to the parking area.

2. **Mount Washburn / Dunraven Pass area** (northeast section). Soaring to an elevation of 10,243 feet, Mount Washburn is the one of the highest points in the park that is easily accessible by roadway. Chittenden Road leads 1.3 miles to a parking area and the north end trailhead to Mount Washburn Trail. This subalpine habitat supports plants that are typically found in northern climates, including a wide assortment of ferns, mosses, and lichens, and wildflowers such as yellow columbine and scarlet monkeyflower. In July, the hillsides burst with color as wildflowers pop up to soak in the warming rays of the sun. The Mount Washburn and Dunraven Pass area is one of the most spectacular areas in the park for breathtaking views and spectacular displays of wildflowers in July and August. Grizzlies, elk, foxes and bighorn sheep are frequently seen on the slopes in the summer. Keep an eye out for red fox, dusky grouse, Clark's nutcracker, chipmunks, whitebark

pine, shooting stars, and paintbrush. Look for high-altitude butterflies. Remember to dress in layers and start your hike in the morning, as thunderstorms are common in the afternoons. Trails are often snow covered until late June.

3. **Hayden Valley** (northeast section). In spring and late summer, the lush grasslands and wetlands of Hayden Valley are prime habitats for spotting migrating waterfowl and shorebirds. Large herds of bison and elk graze in the lush meadows here in spring and fall. During the fall rut, bull bison engage in dusty battles over mating rites. Bison and elk sometimes frequent the trails around Mud Volcano, so remember to keep your distance. At Nez Perce Ford picnic area, you can see waterfowl such as mergansers, goldeneyes, and buffleheads. In spring bring your binoculars to look for a rookery of great blue herons that nest on an island in the river just south of the picnic area. Along the river watch for osprey and bald eagles hunting for fish. In June and July, LeHardy Rapids is a great place to watch for jumping cutthroat trout as they make their way to their spawning waters near Fishing Bridge. Look for harlequin ducks in the rapids. Mushrooms grow along the boardwalk at LeHardy Rapids.

4. **North Entrance / Mammoth Hot Springs area.** Five miles from the North Entrance at Gardiner, Montana, Mammoth is one of the most reliable places to see elk as they leisurely graze and lounge on the grassy lawns around the buildings. Uinta ground squirrels are abundant here, too. As you drive along the road between the North Entrance and Mammoth, watch for pronghorn on the grassy hillsides and bighorn sheep on the tall cliffs. Pinyon jays, lazuli buntings, and magpies hop about the limber pine, Douglas-fir, narrow-leaved cottonwood, and Rocky Mountain juniper that line the banks of the Gardner River. Fragrant sumac, big sagebrush, and black greasewood provide shelter for the white-tailed jackrabbits and Audubon cottontails that you may see scampering across

the road at the entrance station. On a short drive along the Old Yellowstone Road north of Roosevelt Arch, you may find bull snakes and see night hawks, prairie falcons, and cliff swallows zoom overhead. In summer, at the picnic area at the Gardner River, look for American dippers and western tanagers. At night, watch for great horned owls silently hunting over the grassy areas surrounding the Mammoth housing areas. The hike up the Mammoth terraces offers close-up views of the unique otherworldly terraces that have been built from calcium carbonate.

5. **Old Faithful area.** One of the most visited areas in the park, Old Faithful geyser is on the "bucket list" for many people from around the world. The world famous geyser erupts about every 90 minutes, and crowds gather on benches to watch the show. The boardwalk trails that wind through the Upper Geyser Basin also afford the opportunity to see wildlife and special plants such as Rocky Mountain fringed gentian. Mountain bluebirds and western tanagers keep to the borders of the tree line, while opportunistic ravens and Brewer's blackbirds scavenge for food. The microorganisms that grow in the hot geyser fields create an array of colorful texture in the hot streams, while ephydrid flies dance lightly over the edges of the water. Fly fishers can test their casting skills with the brown, rainbow, and brook trout that thrive in the cold, swift waters of the Firehole River. Watch for soaring raptors such as ospreys and red-tailed hawks. Other birds to look for include Canada geese, American robins, and yellow-rumped warblers. Elk, bison, and coyotes may be seen walking across the fields. The best time to avoid crowds at Old Faithful is at dawn or on a moonlit night, when some of the most the dramatic geyser images are taken. At the Lower Geyser Basin you can take the boardwalk trail at Fountain Paint Pots and then a 3-mile drive along Firehole Lake Drive. The nearby Midway Geyser Basin contains Yellowstone's largest hot spring, the stunning Grand Prismatic Spring.

6. **Yellowstone Lake area / Fishing Bridge, Bridge Bay, Gull Point Drive, and Pelican Valley.** At 7,732 feet elevation, and with over 131 square miles of surface area, Yellowstone Lake is the largest freshwater lake above 7,000 feet in the country. Formed by volcanic and glacial activity, the lake reaches a maximum depth of 410 feet. White pelicans, common mergansers, California gulls, western grebe, and Barrow's goldeneye can be seen here. At Bridge Bay, you can make arrangements for a fishing tour or an informative narrated boat cruise on the lake. Even though fishing is no longer permitted from Fishing Bridge, this is a great place to spot wildlife: white pelicans, eagles, ducks, gray jays, trout, and butterflies, including Hayden's ringlet. Near Bridge Bay, Gull Point Drive offers views of waterfowl including lesser scaups, Barrow's goldeneye, bufflehead, and mallards, and keep an eye out for spotted sandpipers. Pelican Valley is famous for abundant wildlife including grizzly bears. Watch for dusky grouse at Lake Butte Overlook. The drive east toward the East Entrance has magnificent wildflower displays in summer.

7. **Grand Canyon of the Yellowstone.** The Upper (109 feet) and Lower Falls (308 feet) of the Yellowstone River plunge over colorful rhyolite cliffs to the canyon floor below. Short hikes to Lookout Point and Inspiration Point give you unprecedented views into the canyon, which is about 20 miles long. On the way keep your eyes peeled for ravens, eagles, and peregrine falcons. Make sure to stop at the Canyon Visitor Education Center for interactive exhibits, audiovisual productions, and interpretive models of Yellowstone's volcanic activities and geological forces that have shaped the park.

8. **Grant / West Thumb.** Known as the quiet side of the park, this peaceful area should not be overlooked for wildlife. At Grant marina keep an eye out for California and ring-billed gulls as well as eagles and pelicans flying by. The Grant

Village campground is a great place to spot snowshoe hares. This area is also a good area to look for colorful mushrooms, dusky grouse, and mule deer. In June, you can see the lovely blooms of glacier lilies and violets.

9. **Blacktail Plateau Drive.** This is a beautiful wildflower area in July with pastel-painted meadows of salmon-colored paint-brush, yellow arnica, white geranium, purple wild onion, and green bog orchids soaking in the short Wyoming summer sun. Butterflies such as common alpine butterfly and little blues bounce from bloom to bloom in the warm breeze. Late afternoon is a good time to look for mule deer and both black and grizzly bears.

10. **Tower-Roosevelt.** At the spectacular Tower Fall, you can see the 132-foot drop of Tower Creek. Columnar basalt cliffs are evident near here. At the Petrified Tree and Specimen Ridge, you can see ancient redwood trees and others turned to stone from volcanic activity. This area is also good for spotting animals including grizzly and black bears, bison, coyote, marmots, peregrine falcons, sandhill cranes, and mountain bluebirds. Climb aboard a stagecoach at Roosevelt Lodge for a narrated ride into the valley, followed by a tasty cookout.

Natural Areas outside Yellowstone National Park

1. **Grand Teton National Park.** Passing from the south boundary of Yellowstone through the John D. Rockefeller Jr. Memorial Parkway on a 7.5-mile-long scenic roadway (US 89/287), you reach Grand Teton National Park, which offers extraordinary wildlife and spectacular scenery. A scenic photographer's dream, the striking Teton Range is the backdrop to pristine lakes, wide rivers, dark green forests, and rolling flower-filled meadows. If you missed seeing a moose in Yellowstone, you have another chance at the Oxbow Bend,

Yellowstone has been called the Serengeti of North America as here you will find the largest concentration of free-roaming wildlife in the Lower 48 states.

where sightings of moose, eagles, black bears, otters, pelicans, and other wildlife are common. The colorful town of Jackson Hole, Wyoming, is just south of the park. ***Note:*** Roads connecting Grand Teton National Park with Yellowstone are closed in winter, and it is about a 2.5-hour drive from West Yellowstone, Montana, via US 20 and US 32 to Jackson Hole, Wyoming. (307) 739-3300; nps.gov/grte.

2. **National Elk Refuge.** Located near Jackson, Wyoming, the grassy meadows and marshes in the National Elk Refuge provide habitat for elk, bison, trumpeter swans, bald eagles, and wolves. With lots of information about the area as well as education programs and interpretive displays, the Jackson Hole & Greater Yellowstone Visitor Center is a wonderful place to visit. 532 North Cache St., Jackson, WY 83001; (307)

733-3316;   fws.gov/nwrs/three
column.aspx?id=2147509813.
In winter, visitors can take a
horse-drawn sleigh ride to see
vast herds of elk up close. 75 E.
Broadway, Jackson, WY 83001;
(307) 733-9212; fws.gov/refuge/
National_Elk_Refuge.

3. **Grizzly and Wolf Discovery Center.** Located just outside the West Entrance to the park in West Yellowstone, Montana, the Grizzly and Wolf Discovery Center is a great place to see wolves and bears up close in a controlled environment. Open daily, this nonprofit wildlife park and educational facility offers visitors a unique opportunity to see some of these top predators in a safe environment. Admission fee. Located one block from the East Entrance of Yellowstone. 201 S. Canyon, West Yellowstone, MT 59758; (406) 646-7001 or (800) 257-2570; grizzlydiscoveryctr.com.

A winter visit to Yellowstone offers quiet solitude as well as unique opportunities to view wildlife.

4. **Museum of the Rockies.** Located in Bozeman, Montana, about a 90-minute drive north of Yellowstone, this world-class museum houses one of the largest dinosaur collections in the world. Here you can also take a look at some of the cultural history and a planetarium. Admission fee. 600 W. Kagy Blvd., Bozeman, MT 59717; (406) 994-2251; museum oftherockies.org/Home.aspx.

5. **Beartooth Highway.** A National Scenic Byway All-American Road, the Beartooth Highway is celebrated as one of the

The cold, clear waters of Yellowstone provide exciting fly-fishing opportunities.

most scenic drives in the west. Connecting the Northeast Entrance of Yellowstone with Red Lodge, Montana, via US 212, the Beartooth Highway offers breathtaking views of the Absaroka and Beartooth Mountains. The roadway winds 68 miles over the Beartooth Pass at an elevation of 10,977 feet through one of the most significant high-alpine ecosystems accessible by vehicle in the United States. Wildlife-viewing opportunities abound as the Custer, Gallatin, and Shoshone National Forests surround the road. Along the way, watch for bears, moose, mountain goats, elk, and mule deer. Make sure to purchase fuel before beginning your journey, as there are limited services here. From Cody, Wyoming, you can travel on WY 120 for 17 miles to the junction of WY 120 and WY 296 on the Chief Joseph Scenic Highway for 47 miles to join the Beartooth Highway (US 212). Generally open Memorial Day weekend to mid-October. Red Lodge Chamber of Commerce, (406) 446-1718; beartoothhighway.com.

6. **Glacier National Park.** About an 8-hour drive from the North Entrance of Yellowstone to West Glacier, Montana, brings you to Glacier National Park. Glacier is a land of rugged mountains, glacially carved valleys, alpine meadows filled with colorful wildflowers, spectacular lakes, and pristine forests. Not to be missed is the jaw-dropping scenic drive along the 50-mile-long Going-to-the-Sun Road that is normally open mid-June to mid-September. Along the road, and especially near Logan Pass, watch for mountain goats and bighorn sheep as well as grizzly and black bears. Note some vehicle restrictions are in place. For more information call (406) 888-7800 or log on to nps.gov/glac. While visiting Glacier, consider a visit to its sister park, Waterton Lakes National Park in Canada (passport required): (403) 859-5133 or pc.gc.ca/eng/pn-np/ab/waterton/index.aspx. Together, these two parks make up the Waterton-Glacier International Peace Park.

7. **Craters of the Moon National Monument & Preserve.** Located near Arco, Idaho, which is about a 3.5-hour drive from the West Entrance of Yellowstone, Craters of the Moon National Monument & Preserve has a 7-mile-loop road winding through rugged landscape formed from past lava flows. Along the drive, you can spot mule deer, ground squirrels, marmots, and sage grouse. (208) 527-1335; nps.gov/crmo.

8. **Bighorn Canyon National Recreation Area.** Home to bighorn sheep, wild horses, mule deer, black bears, and mountain lions, Bighorn Canyon National Recreation Area is a great place to see wildlife. Located near Lovell, Wyoming, about a 2-hour drive from the East Entrance to Yellowstone, Bighorn Canyon has one of the most unique landscapes in the west. (307) 548-5406;nps.gov/bica.

9. **Devils Tower National Monument.** Located about a 7-hour drive from Yellowstone's East Entrance, Devils Tower National Monument is an unusual geologic feature standing in the middle of the rolling prairie surrounding the Black Hills. Hundreds of parallel cracks in igneous rock make this a climber's mecca. This is also a mecca for black-tailed prairie dogs, and these entertaining ground lovers are abundant here. The monument has long been considered a place of spiritual and cultural importance for American Indians. The 1977 science fiction movie *Close Encounters of the Third Kind* was filmed here. (307) 467-5283; nps.gov/deto.

Ecosystems

Yellowstone National Park is in the heart of what is known as the Greater Yellowstone Ecosystem (GYE). This 28,000-square-mile area encompasses Yellowstone National Park's 2.2 million acres and is one of the most important biodiversity areas in North America. Included within the GYE boundaries are three states:

Yellowstone provides habitat protection for great gray owls to raise their young.

Wyoming, Montana, and Idaho. Within the GYE, both Yellowstone and Grand Teton National Parks provide sanctuary for the largest concentration of wildlife in the Lower 48 states. The surrounding land includes portions of five national forests and three national wildlife refuges. Underlain by volcanic bedrock, most of the park is above 7,500 feet in elevation. The northern range includes sagebrush steppe and grasslands that provide important winter habitat for elk, bison, and bighorn sheep.

The geothermal wonders and colorful thermophiles of Yellowstone are unique in the world.

Park rangers offer a wealth of knowledge about natural history in Yellowstone through educational programs.

Geology

Yellowstone's landscape has been carved, eroded, and formed from many geological forces. The area that is now Yellowstone has been covered by glaciers many times. The last glacier left behind large boulders called glacial erratics, which can be seen today in areas such as Tower Fall and in Lamar and Hayden Valleys. Located on top of an active volcano, the many hydrothermal features of Yellowstone prompted the decision to make this area the world's first national park. The volcano underlying the park is considered a "supervolcano" capable of erupting more than 240 cubic miles of magma. A land of earthquakes, bubbling mud pots, steaming geysers, hot springs, fumaroles, and travertine terraces, Yellowstone preserves this collection of over 10,000 hydrothermal features. The most famous geyser in the world, Old Faithful, erupts about 17 times per day, but its eruptions range from 60 to 110 minutes. Norris Geyser Basin is the most dynamic of all Yellowstone's active hydrothermal areas. You can see the rim of the Yellowstone Caldera (30 by 45 miles across) best from the Washburn Hot Springs overlook just south of Dunraven Pass. Scientists from the Yellowstone Volcano Observatory constantly monitor earthquakes and volcanic activity (volcanoes.usgs.gov/observatories/yvo/).

Some Examples of Geological Features in Yellowstone

Geyser	Travertine Terrace	Fumarole	Mud Pot	Hot Spring	Columnar Basalt
Old Faithful	Mammoth Hot Springs	Roaring Mountain	Fountain Paint Pot	West Thumb	Sheepeater Cliff
Riverside		Black Growler Steam Vent in Norris Geyser Basin	Artist Paint Pots	Crested Pool	Between Tower Fall and Tower Junction
Castle			West Thumb Geyser Basin		

GOLDEN-MANTLED GROUND SQUIRREL
Spermophilus lateralis
Squirrel family (Sciuridae)
Quick ID: golden reddish-brown; whitish belly; black and white stripes on back; no stripes on head; white ring around eye
Length: 9.5–11.5" Weight: 6–12 oz

With quick movements and bold stripes on its back, the golden-mantled ground squirrel resembles an overgrown chipmunk. Classified as a true squirrel, the key to identifying this chipmunk look-alike from true chipmunks is the lack of stripes on the head and a white ring around the eye. The broad back stripes begin at the shoulders, while those of a chipmunk begin near its cheeks. Also, chipmunks are much smaller, only reaching about 8 inches, while the golden-mantled ground squirrel can reach over 11 inches in length. These lively squirrels are named for the russet golden "mantle" on their neck and shoulders. Found throughout the park, golden-mantled ground squirrels are nearly omnivorous, as they eat a wide variety of foods including insects, fungi, seeds, and other plants.

UINTA GROUND SQUIRREL
Urocitellus armatus
Squirrel family (Sciuridae)
Quick ID: brownish-gray with white specks, nose and shoulders rufous; short 2.5–3" tail
Length: 11–12" Weight: 6.9–10.4 oz

Like their distant prairie-dog cousins, for whom they are sometimes mistaken, Uinta ground squirrels form loose social groups in open areas. If a threat approaches, they produce alarm calls to warn their family members, who quickly scamper into their underground burrows. Mammoth Hot Springs is one of the best places in the park to observe Uinta ground squirrels as they entertain visitors with their busy foraging activities. Only active for about 4 months during the year, they begin to emerge from their underground burrows in April and return underground by August. During this short time, they pay for their long seasonal naps by working constantly to gather and store grasses and other plant materials for the winter.

RED SQUIRREL
Tamiasciurus hudsonicus
Squirrel family (Sciuridae)
Quick ID: reddish-brown; creamy white underneath; large black eyes with whitish eye ring; no stripes on back; long 4–6" reddish-brown tail edged with black and white
Length: 11–13.7" Weight: 6–11 oz

The fearless terriers of the squirrel world, red squirrels loudly scold intruders who come near their territory with high-pitched barking and chattering. These animated threats may include tail-flicking, foot stomping, and racing along branches. Also known as pine squirrels or chickarees, these vocal forest sentinels are larger than chipmunks but smaller than ground squirrels. Like the golden-mantled ground squirrel, *Spermophilus lateralis*, the red squirrel has a white ring around the eye, but red squirrels lack any stripes on the back. Quite industrious, red squirrels busily spend the day gathering conifer cones that they store in caches called middens. Growing larger each year, the middens may be several feet deep and 15 feet wide. Red squirrels also gather mushrooms that they wedge between branches to dry for winter use.

LEAST CHIPMUNK
Tamias minimus
Squirrel family (Sciuridae)
Quick ID: very small; rusty-gray; 5 dark and 4 pale stripes on back and face; pale gray spots behind brown ears; tawny rump; 4" buffy orange tail; underparts white
Length: 7.5–8.5"   Weight: 1.2–1.9 oz

Aptly named, the least chipmunk is the smallest member of the squirrel family. Chipmunks nervously dart about with their tails held high in the air as they search for seeds and other food, which they store in underground burrows. In Greek, the genus name, *Tamias*, means "one who stores provisions." Two larger chipmunks, yellowpine chipmunks, *T. amoenus*, and Uinta chipmunks, *Neotamias umbrinus*, can be found in Yellowstone. Sometimes confused with golden-mantled ground squirrels, chipmunks can be distinguished by their smaller size and by stripes on their face, which are lacking in golden-mantled ground squirrels. According to an American Indian legend, chipmunks got their back stripes from marks left by a bear's claws as punishment for teasing and making fun of others.

NORTHERN FLYING SQUIRREL
Glaucomys sabrinus
Squirrel family (Sciuridae)
Quick ID: buffy-gray; large black eyes; grayish-white underneath; 4.9–6.0" flattened tail; furred membrane between front and back legs
Length: 10.8–13.4"   Weight: 2.6–4.9 oz

Some of nature's most elusive creatures are actually quite active but rarely seen as they spend their waking hours under cover of darkness. The northern flying squirrel is one of these nocturnal animals that many people don't even know exists. In spite of its name, this small mammal never flies; instead they have a furred fold of skin between the front legs and the back legs that allows spectacular glides between trees of up to 90 feet in length. These night lovers have large eyes that gather lots of available light as they forage for lichens, seeds, nuts, tree sap, and insects. The favorite food of these superhero squirrels is a fungus called a truffle. A delicacy for humans as well, truffles are underground mushrooms that the squirrels locate by smell.

YELLOW-BELLIED MARMOT
Marmota flaviventris
Squirrel family (Sciuridae)
Quick ID: grizzled reddish-brown on back; yellowish belly; short bushy tail; small ears; whitish band across nose
Length: 1.5–2.2' Weight: 3.3–8.8 lb

You may hear their high-pitched chucks, whistles, and trills before you see them, but yellow-bellied marmots can be found leisurely sunning themselves on rocky ledges throughout the park. Closely related to the groundhog found in the eastern states, the yellow-bellied marmot is native to western states. Marmots eat a wide variety of vegetation, and by fall, they accumulate enough fat reserves to keep them alive during their long winter hibernation. One of the best ways to enjoy seeing these roly-poly inhabitants of Yellowstone is on an excellent wagon ride from Roosevelt corral that passes a rocky area fondly referred to as "marmot apartments or hotel." Other places to spot marmots in the park include Observation Point, which overlooks Old Faithful and the Upper Geyser Basin, Sheepeater Cliff, and the Mount Washburn area.

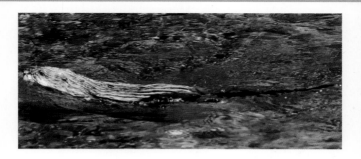

COMMON MUSKRAT
Ondatra zibethicus
Mice, rat, and vole family (Cricetidae)
Quick ID: glossy brown; robust body; laterally flattened scaly tail; small eyes; short legs; webbed hind feet
Length: 16–24" Weight: 1.5–3.9 lb

Aptly named for their resemblance to big rats as well as the strong musky odor they produce, muskrats mark their territories using scent glands. Found in marshy areas, ponds, streams, and wetlands, the muskrat has webbed hind feet and a rudder-like tail that helps them maneuver through their habitat. Even though muskrats are similar in appearance and habitat to beavers, they are much smaller, weigh much less, and have a long, narrow tail rather than the flattened paddle-like tail of the beaver. In addition, muskrats lack the strong chisel-like teeth of beavers; therefore, they cannot gnaw through trees. Look for muskrats in wet areas in the park including the Firehole River near Old Faithful and the Yellowstone River.

SOUTHERN RED-BACKED VOLE
Myodes gapperi
Mice, rat, and vole family (Cricetidae)
Quick ID: tiny, mouse-like; rusty-gray; pale underparts; short 1.1–1.9" tail
Length: 2.76–4.41" Weight: 0.21–1.48 oz

Although tiny in size, voles are one of most important members of the food chain. With one of the highest reproductive rates among mammals, voles are capable of mating at 3 months of age. The constantly productive females have 2 or 3 litters of 1–11 young during the year. With such a high reproductive rate, the population of voles would soon overrun the habitat if they were not the favorite food of many predators, including coyotes and great gray owls. The genus name, *Myodes*, comes from the Greek for "keyhole mouse," and the species name, *gapperi*, is to honor a British physician, Dr. Anthony Gapper (1799–1883), who studied voles in Canada.

DEER MOUSE
Peromyscus maniculatus
Mice, rat, and vole family (Cricetidae)
Quick ID: grayish- to reddish-brown; white underparts; white feet; long bicolored 2–5"
tail, dark on top and lighter on bottom; large beady eyes; large round ears
Length: 2.8–4" Weight: 0.66–1.25 oz

Deer mice don't hang around with deer, nor do they act like deer, but these tiny creatures do have the same color hair as deer, hence their common name. Like a deer, their backs are brownish with white on their legs and belly. Even their tails are similar, with dark brown on the top and white underneath. Deer mice are common in Yellowstone, but they are active mainly at night and therefore not often seen. Deer mice can produce 2–4 litters per year typically with 3–5 young. An important foundation in the ecological food chain, these and other rodents are an important source of protein for a wide variety of predators, including hawks, owls, and coyotes.

AMERICAN BEAVER
Castor canadensis
Beaver family (Castoridae)
Quick ID: dark brown, coarse fur; broad, flat, paddle-shaped tail; small rounded ears; wedge-shaped head
Length: 3–3.9' Weight: 35–50 lb

Widely recognized by their large, flat paddle-shaped tail, the American beaver holds the honor of being the largest rodent in North America. Active at night, these natural engineers use their large chisel-like teeth to cut down saplings and construct dams and lodges in streams, making their own private swimming area and home. Adept at conserving oxygen, they can remain submerged for 15 minutes. Beavers have a unique digestive system that allows them to eat and digest bark and the inner layer of wood under the bark called cambium. They have a symbiotic relationship with microorganisms in their intestines that digest cellulose. Watch for these aquatic specialists in the Yellowstone, Madison, and Gallatin Rivers and in the Slough Creek area.

NORTH AMERICAN PORCUPINE
Erethizon dorsatum
Porcupine family (Erethizontidae)
Quick ID: brownish; chunky body, arching back; yellowish 5" quills
Length: 24–51" Weight: 7.7–39.6 lb

In a unique example of survival in the natural world, the hairs of the North American porcupine have evolved into an exceptional defense system. This slow-moving woodland inhabitant has a soft underbelly but defends itself with 30,000 barbed quills on its back and short tail. Contrary to popular myth, porcupines cannot throw their quills, but the hollow quills readily detach when brushed up against a solid object. The waxy quills are tipped with tiny barbs that inflict a painful stab to the attacker, making removal difficult. During the day, porcupines rest in trees or brushy areas; at night they forage for vegetation and the inner bark of trees. Porcupine quills were used by American Indians as decorative additions to clothing and other items.

NORTHERN POCKET GOPHER
Thomomys talpoides
Pocket gopher family (Geomyidae)
Quick ID: guinea-pig-like; brownish-tan; rounded muzzle; short 2", nearly hairless tail; tiny eyes; small ears; long front claws
Length: 6.5–10.2" Weight: 2.1–5.6 oz

For a creature that lives most of its life underground, gophers are surprisingly successful at making a living. Born to dig, northern pocket gophers use their long front claws and their sturdy front teeth to excavate extensive tunnels, moving over a ton of soil to the surface each year.

Feeding on roots, bulbs, stems, and leaves of plants, they use their expandable fur-lined cheek pouches as "pockets" to transport food to underground storage tunnels. These excavation activities benefit soil quality, improve habitat for plants, and help prevent erosion. Their winter tunnels through snow are often filled with soil, leaving long snakelike mounds called gopher eskers. Fossil records trace these subterranean rodents back 3–5 million years, to the Pliocene epoch.

AMERICAN PIKA
Ochotona princeps
Pika family (Ochotonidae)
Quick ID: grayish-brown; guinea-pig-like; small, rounded, white-edged ears; short legs
Length: 6.5–8.5" Weight: 4–6.5 oz

You will probably hear the high-pitched single "beep" call before you see this tiny rock climber that lives in colonies amid boulder fields. Resembling cuddly gerbils or small guinea pigs, these tiny high-country inhabitants are related to rabbits. Sensitive to high temperatures, pikas must move higher in altitude to stay cool enough for survival in the summer. Pika may be one of the mammals most threatened by global warming, as they can't survive in temperatures above 80°F. The word *pika* comes from a Russian word for "squeak." As they do not hibernate, in the summer these tiny survivors busily gather vegetation to dry and then store in hay piles for the long winter. Look for pika on rocky slopes near Tower and south of Mammoth.

WHITE-TAILED JACKRABBIT
Lepus townsendii
Hare and rabbit family (Leporidae)
Quick ID: brown in summer, white in winter; large ears; large feet; long legs
Length: 18–22" Weight: 5–10 lb

Dashing back and forth across the road, white-tailed jackrabbits amuse the rangers that staff the park entrance gate near Gardiner, Montana. Hiding under cover most of the day, these speedsters are equipped with large 6-inch ears to alert them to predators such as coyotes. Their oversize hind legs, which facilitate high jumps and lightning sprints, match skills with larger predators. Like the similar, but smaller, snowshoe hares, *L. americanus*, the brown coat of white-tailed jackrabbits turns white during the winter to aid in camouflage. Residing in coniferous forests, snowshoe hares may be seen at Grant Village campground in the Madison area. White-tailed jackrabbits can also be seen in the Mammoth campground.

MOUNTAIN COTTONTAIL
Sylvilagus nuttallii
Rabbit and hare family (Leporidae)
Quick ID: small; pale gray–brown rabbit; black-tipped ears; pale brown nape on back of head
Length: 13.3–15.3" Weight: 1.4–1.9 lb

Peeking out from under boardwalks of Mammoth Hot Springs and Mammoth campground, mountain cottontails watch carefully for predators including coyotes, red-tail hawks, and owls. Also known as Nuttall's cottontail, the mountain cottontail is very similar to the dessert cottontail, *S. audubonii*, which is also found in the park. The genus name, *Sylvilagus*, means "rabbit of the forest," and the species name, *nuttallii*, was given to this rabbit to honor Thomas Nuttall, a botanist and naturalist explorer of the early 1800s. Active mainly at dawn and dusk, when startled they bound away, flagging their white tails to warn others, but then quickly stop and seemingly disappear in perfect camouflage with the surrounding grasses and shrubs.

49

DUSKY SHREW
Sorex monticolus
Shrew family (Soricidae)
Quick ID: silvery-gray; mouselike; long nose; sharp peg-like teeth; small indistinguishable ears; small eyes; 1.5–2.4" tail
Length: 3.7–5.4"   Weight: 0.15–0.35 oz

The dusky, or montane, shrew is one of 5 species of shrews that can be found in the Yellowstone region. Dusky shrews are insectivores eating a variety insects, spiders, and worms. The envy of dieters, the metabolic rate of shrews is so high that they eat about 85 percent of their body weight daily to maintain their weight. Some species of shrews, such as the American water shrew, *S. palustris*, are venomous and can inject venom through grooves in their teeth. Shrew venom is currently being studied for its medicinal purposes. Nagging people are sometimes referred to as shrews, stemming from the Middle English word *shrewe*, meaning a mean-spirited or scolding person. Although rarely seen, dusky shrews can be found in moist meadows and forested areas often near water such as LeHardy Rapids.

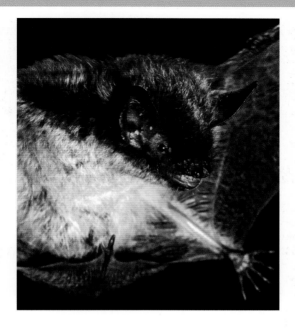

LITTLE BROWN BAT
Myotis lucifugus
Bat family (Vespertilionidae)
Quick ID: glossy brown; buffy belly; small rounded ears
Length: 3.1–3.7" Weight: 0.19–0.42 oz

Of all the magnificent mammals in Yellowstone, the bat is one of the most important but least appreciated. One of the most common bats in Yellowstone, and in all of North America, is the little brown bat. Racing through the air on wings that span about 8.5–10.5 inches, this flying dive bomber can snatch up over 1,200 insects in an hour's work. The park is home to about 8 species of bats that play a pivotal role in insect control, including gnats, mosquitoes, moths, and beetles. Bats roost in protected areas such as trees, caves, and buildings. Biologists are keeping a careful watch on bats for a deadly fungal disease called white-nose syndrome that has swept through many hibernating bat colonies, causing a severe decline in several species.

BOBCAT
Lynx rufus
Cat family (Felidae)
Quick ID: tawny to gray with black spots and bars; ear tufts; short tail with black tip on top and white underneath
Length: 2.2–3.75' Weight: 11–33 lb

Although bobcats are not commonly found in Yellowstone because of the prohibitively deep snow that covers the park in winter, these small felines have been sighted in the northern section of the park. Their dark markings, short bobbed tail, and relatively small size help to identify this member of the cat family from the larger lynx, which is also found in the park. Active mainly at dawn and dusk, bobcats have a keen sense of sight and smell that helps them locate prey such as rodents, squirrels, and other small mammals. They seek shelter for rest and sleep in hollow trees, rock piles, and brush piles. Solitary animals, bobcats communicate their territory by scent marking and scratching on a tree or log.

COUGAR
Puma concolor
Cat family (Felidae)
Quick ID: uniform tawny brown with no spots (except when young), whitish underparts,
very long (25–35") black-tipped tail
Length: 6–8' Weight: 88–220 lb

Recovering slowly from a widespread predator removal campaign in the
early 1900s, only about 14–23 adult cougars live today within the boundaries of the rugged northern range of Yellowstone National Park. Cougars
prey mainly on elk and deer but will take other small animals such as
squirrels and rabbits. During the last ice age, cougars survived by eating
a wide variety of prey, becoming one of the most widely dispersed animals in the Western Hemisphere, at one time living in every eastern state.
Rarely seen, cougars normally avoid human contact, but as people enter
their habitat, encounters are inevitable. Do not let children run ahead of
you on trails. If attacked, pick up children and fight back. Do not hike,
bike, or jog alone, especially at dawn, dusk, or night.

CANADA LYNX
Lynx canadensis
Cat family (Felidae)
Quick ID: grayish-brown, mottled with white and buffy brown; black 1" ear tufts; short tail with complete rings and solid black tip; hind legs longer than front legs
Length: 26–33" Weight: 16–35 lb

The elusive lynx is at home in the rugged mountains of Yellowstone and the surrounding ecosystem. Though uncommon, they have been spotted in the northeast corner of the park and near Yellowstone Lake. Their favorite prey is snowshoe hares, which are found in the park in low numbers; in the park, lynx may make more use of prey such as squirrels, rodents, and grouse. Lynx are similar to bobcats but are larger with longer legs. The tip of a lynx's tail is entirely black, whereas the underside of a bobcat's tail is white. Also, the back of the hind legs is light beige on the lynx and black on the bobcat. Mountain lions are larger than both lynx and bobcat, and they have a much longer tail and body.

COYOTE
Canis latrans
Dog family (Canidae)
Quick ID: medium size, doglike; gray to reddish coat mixed with tan, brown, and black; pointed, erect ears; long, slender snout; black-tipped tail usually carried straight down
Length: 2.5–3.3' (body)   Weight: 25–40 lb

Along with foxes and wolves, coyotes occur historically throughout the Yellowstone ecosystem. Coyotes are extremely versatile and are able to adjust quickly to a wide variety of habitats and circumstances. This hardy and adaptable canine feeds mainly on voles, pocket gophers, ground squirrels, and elk but will supplement their diets with fruit and plant materials. Coyotes will also take advantage of carrion, especially the remains of wolf kills, where they compete with ravens, eagles, and magpies for the leftovers. Often misidentified as a wolf, a coyote is about one-third the size of a wolf and has a slender, pointed snout, unlike the wider, boxy face and snout of a wolf. The most commonly seen canine, coyotes can be spotted in every part of the park.

GRAY WOLF
Canis lupus
Dog family (Canidae)
Quick ID: varied from mottled gray with brown to black or white; broad head and muzzle; long legs; short, rounded ears
Length: 2.8–4.2' (body)   Weight: 70–120 lb

After many silent years, visitors to Yellowstone National Park can once again hear the enthralling chorus of wolf howls resounding through the mountains and valleys. After a successful reintroduction program in 1995, these top predators are once again playing an integral role in maintaining the ecological balance in Yellowstone. As they have done for thousands of years, wolves prey mainly on elk, deer, bison, and small mammals. Sometimes called timber wolves, most gray wolves in Yellowstone are characteristically gray, but other color phases include black and whitish. Highly social, approximately 90 wolves live in about 10 packs in Yellowstone. Bring your binoculars and spotting scopes and head out early in the morning to look for wolves in Lamar Valley, the Slough Creek area, and Hayden Valley.

Comparison of Canids in Yellowstone

	Gray Wolf	Coyote	Red Fox
Comparative size	Large	Medium	Small
Comparative dog-breed size	Great Dane (wolf weighs about the same)	Golden retriever (but coyote weighs less)	Cocker spaniel (but fox weighs less)
Color	Variable: grizzled gray, black, whitish	Gray to reddish with mix of tan, brown, black	Rusty red above (variable), white underneath, black legs
Head shape	Blocky, squarish	Narrow, triangular	Narrow, triangular
Snout	Broad, blocky	Long, slender	Slender, pointed
Length (nose to tail)	5–6'	3.6–4.6'	3.3–4.9'
Height (at shoulder)	27–33"	20–22"	15–16"
Weight	70–120 lb	25–40 lb	7–15 lb
Length of front foot	About 3.6" or more	About 2.7" or less	About 2.3"
Ears	Short, rounded; relatively small	Tall, pointed; relatively medium	Triangular, pointed, erect; relatively large
Tail length	14–2.3"	12–15"	14–16.6"
Tail	Sometimes black tipped; usually carried horizontally or high	Usually black tipped; usually carried down	White tipped; usually carried horizontally

RED FOX
Vulpes vulpes
Dog family (Canidae)
Quick ID: small, doglike; variable reddish coat, white underneath; white-tipped, bushy tail; black behind pointed ears
Length: 2.7–3.6' (body) Weight: 7–15 lb

Known worldwide for their cunning intelligence, red foxes are one of the most adaptable and opportunistic of all wild dog species. Able to survive in a variety of habitats, foxes prefer small mammals but will also eat fruit, insects, fish, and amphibians. Their excellent hearing allows them to locate small rodents, such as voles, beneath the snow. Springing into the air, foxes leap in a headfirst snow dive to catch their prey. In Yellowstone, red foxes prefer forested areas, especially Douglas-fir habitats, but in winter they may move into sagebrush habitats for hunting. Primarily nocturnal, foxes are not seen as often as coyotes. At dawn and dusk, look for foxes in the Mount Washburn area, Lamar Valley, and the northeast corner of the park.

BLACK BEAR
Ursus americanus
Bear family (Ursidae)
Quick ID: variable black to brownish, blond, or cinnamon; straight, brownish snout; rump higher than shoulders without prominent shoulder hump
Length: 4'6"–6'2" Weight: 135–315 lb

Ranging across the northern states and Canada to the East Coast, black bears share the forests of Yellowstone with their larger grizzly cousins. Along with Old Faithful, black bears became symbols of the park as visitors enjoyed watching them eat from garbage dumps and accepting handouts along the road. This practice resulted in unnecessary property damage and many unfortunate human injuries. Today, visitors in the park are required to safely store their food, use bear-proof garbage containers, and never attempt to feed bears. Black bears in Yellowstone can range in coloration from black to blond or cinnamon, which sometimes causes misidentification as a grizzly. Look for black bears throughout the park but especially in Lamar and Hayden Valleys, and near Tower Fall, Mammoth Hot Springs, and Specimen Ridge area.

GRIZZLY BEAR
Ursus arctos
Bear family (Ursidae)
Quick ID: brownish (variable) with silvery-tipped hair; hump above shoulders; dish-shaped face; rounded ears
Length: 6'3"–7'9" Weight: 200–700 lb

A majestic symbol of the wild, the grizzly bear is a subspecies of the brown bear commonly found in Alaska and Canada. Of the nearly 600 grizzlies that inhabit the Greater Yellowstone Ecosystem, only about 150 of these call Yellowstone National Park their home. Sometimes confused with black bears, the adult grizzly is larger, with a dished face and a prominent shoulder hump. Certain high-density grizzly areas in the park are seasonally restricted or closed, so make sure to check at a visitor center for current information. At dawn or dusk, the best places to see grizzlies in the park include Lamar and Hayden Valleys, Mount Washburn / Dunraven Pass, Fishing Bridge area to the East Entrance, Swan Lake Flat, Yellowstone Lake, and in the northeast section of the park.

Comparison of Black Bears and Grizzly Bears

	Black Bear	Grizzly Bear
Color	Varies between black, brown, blonde, and cinnamon	Grizzled brown (varied shades of brown)
Shoulder	No prominent shoulder hump	Prominent shoulder hump
Rump	Higher than shoulders	Lower than shoulders
Face profile	Straight face profile; convex profile	Dished face profile; concave profile
Ears	Tall semi-tapered ears; less heavily furred	Short, rounded ears; heavily furred
Back paw	7" long	10" long
Claws (front paws)	Short claws, 1–2"; more curved	Long claws, 2–4"; less curved
Weight (male)	210–315 lb	200–700 lb
Weight (female)	135–200 lb	200–499 lb
Length	5–6'	6'3"–7'9"
Height at shoulder (avg)	2–3'	3–3.5'

LONG-TAILED WEASEL
Mustela frenata
Weasel, skunk, and otter family (Mustelidae)
Quick ID: long, thin brown body; flattened triangular head; long neck; short legs; yellow-ish belly; brownish feet; 3–6" black-tipped tail; rounded ears; fur turns white in winter
Length: 11–16.5" Weight: 2.8–15.8 oz

A long, sinuous brown body, long neck, and rounded ears atop a triangu-lar head are characteristics to help identify a weasel. Sometimes confused with the ermine or short-tailed weasel, *M. erminea*, which is also found in the park, the long-tailed weasel is aptly named, as the 3- to 6-inch, black-tipped tail is often one-third as long as the body. In winter, both species molt in white hairs that blend well with the snow and help camouflage them from both predators and prey. Weasels prey on small mammals such as mice, voles, pocket gophers, and ground squirrels. In folklore, the wea-sel represents a variety of characters, including the mischievous trickster, clever magician, and purveyor of both good and bad luck.

AMERICAN MARTEN
Martes americana
Weasel, skunk, and otter family (Mustelidae)
Quick ID: weasel-like with pointed face and rounded ears; brownish; head and belly paler;
buffy-orange chest or throat; long bushy tail
Length: 19.5–26.5" Weight: 0.6–2.7 lb

Commonly called the pine marten, the American marten is a member of
the weasel family. About the size of a small house cat, this small predator hunts insects, rodents, and other small mammals. It is a lucky day
if you happened to spot a marten, as they are well camouflaged and not
often seen. Small birds may sound alarm notes when a marten is close by,
so if you are observant, you may be fortunate to spot a marten moving
silently through the forests, often loping along a fallen log or racing up
trees. Mostly nocturnal, you can look for these curious forest inhabitants
in spruce-fir forests such as Upper Barronette or rocky areas like Sheepeater Cliff.

AMERICAN BADGER
Taxidea taxus
Weasel, skunk, and otter family (Mustelidae)
Quick ID: grayish-brown; flat, heavy body; short legs; white stripe on middle of dark head, neck, and nose; short bushy tail; shaggy grizzled fur; cream underneath
Length: 2–2.6' Weight: 8–26 lb

Built like a barreling tank, the American badger possesses all of the tenacity and ferocity necessary for survival in Yellowstone. This excavating dynamo has short, powerful legs and long, curved claws perfect for unearthing hideaways in the ground to hunt for rodents and other prey. About the size of a medium- to large-size bulldog, a badger has coarse, grizzled-gray hairs covering its flat body. Its white cheeks sport blackish patches, and a distinctive white stripe is emblazoned on the head and shoulders. Mostly nocturnal, badgers may be spotted waddling into their underground burrows in Lamar Valley and in the area surrounding Old Faithful. Badgers are sometimes mistaken for the rare wolverine, *Gulo gulo*, which resembles a small, short-legged brown bear with buffy sides and a shaggy tail.

NORTHERN RIVER OTTER
Lontra canadensis
Weasel, skunk, and otter family
(Mustelidae)
Quick ID: rich brown fur; elongated cylindrical
body; thick neck; broad head; round tail;
webbed feet; short stubby legs
Length: 2.9–4.3' Weight: 11–30 lb

Playful otters are one of the most amusing animals to watch as they frolic in rivers and creeks in Yellowstone. Superb swimmers, their webbed feet and rudder-like tails help them catch darting fish and other underwater prey. Otters are sometimes confused with other brown animals that live in aquatic habitats. Beavers have a broader, chunkier body and a flattened tail. The streamlined muskrat has a body length of about 1 foot long, while that of an otter is well over 2 feet long. At about 20 pounds, otters are heavyweights when compared with the lightweight muskrats that weigh in at about 3 pounds. Otters are mostly nocturnal, but at dusk or dawn, they may be seen at Trout Lake, Hayden Valley, or at the confluence of Soda Butte Creek and the Lamar River.

FISHER
Martes pennanti
Weasel, skunk, and otter family (Mustelidae)
Quick ID: stocky; weasel-like; rich brown fur; silvery-gold sheen on face and shoulders; short, black legs; 12–16" heavily furred black tail; short round ears
Length: 2.4–3.9' Weight: 4.4–12.1 lbs

Resembling a large, chunky American marten, fishers are one of the larger members of the weasel family. The name is misleading, as these forest animals generally do not prey on fish but favor hares, squirrels, porcupines, rodents, shrews, voles, and carrion. Fishers are larger than American martens but smaller than a wolverine. Highly prized for their thick, silky fur, fishers were hunted to near extinction in the early 20th century, but conservation and reintroduction efforts have fortified populations of these animals. Like the wolverine, fishers are generally solitary and rarely seen. Hikers in mountainous areas, such as the Absaroka Mountain Range near the Northeast Entrance, should keep their eyes open for these elusive predators that require large tracts of forested areas away from developed areas.

MULE DEER
Odocoileus hemionus
Deer family (Cervidae)
Quick ID: grayish-brown to reddish-brown; large mule-like ears; white rump patch; 4–8"
white tail with black-tip; male has forked antlers in fall
Length: 4.1–5.5' Weight: 100–250 lb

Also known as black-tailed deer or "mulies," the mule deer earned its
name from the resemblance of its oversize ears to those of a mule. The
antlers of male mule deer fork and then fork again, while females lack antlers. Smaller than its elk cousins, the mule deer also has a whitish rump
patch but longer black-tipped tail. Pronghorns also have a white rump
patch but a stubbed tail. Mule deer and pronghorns bound away from
danger in a stiff-legged hop called "stotting." The even smaller white-
tailed deer, *O. virginianus*, sometimes wander into park boundaries but
are more typically seen north of Gardiner, Montana. Mule deer can be
spotted at Mammoth and other areas of the park, including the Grant
Village area, Lamar and Hayden Valleys, and Blacktail Deer Plateau.

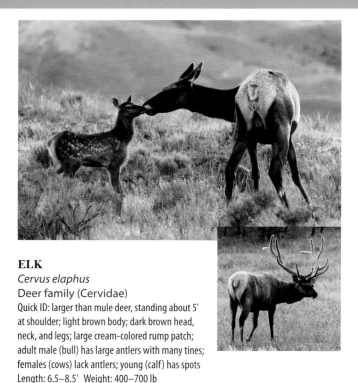

ELK
Cervus elaphus
Deer family (Cervidae)
Quick ID: larger than mule deer, standing about 5'
at shoulder; light brown body; dark brown head,
neck, and legs; large cream-colored rump patch;
adult male (bull) has large antlers with many tines;
females (cows) lack antlers; young (calf) has spots
Length: 6.5–8.5' Weight: 400–700 lb

As the most abundant large mammal in the park, 10,000–20,000 elk spend their summers grazing the lush meadows. In winter, about 75 percent migrate either north to the northern range near Gardiner, Montana, or south to Jackson Hole and the National Elk Refuge near Jackson, Wyoming. During the fall mating season (called the rut), the bugling of bulls can be heard for miles. The hormone-amped bulls are particularly active and may battle other rival bulls with antlers that can reach nearly 6 feet across and weigh about 30–40 pounds per pair. This period is especially dangerous for visitors, as the elk have been known to attack anything that gets too close, even vehicles. Elk may be seen throughout the park but reliably at Mammoth Hot Springs.

MOOSE
Alces alces
Deer family (Cervidae)
Quick ID: large; dark brown; 5.6–7.6' at shoulder; horselike, large bulbous "nose"; dewlap under throat; males have large, flattened palmate antlers
Length: 8–10' Weight: 600–1,000 lb

Moose are easily recognized by their large size and long bulbous nose. Males, called bulls, sport large, flattened antlers through fall but shed them in winter. The antlers may span 6 feet across and weigh up to 70 pounds. Females, called cows, never grow antlers and are smaller than males. Born in late May or June, a newborn moose calf may weigh up to 35 pounds. Moose prefer areas with willow thickets and along streams and marshes. In Yellowstone, look for moose in the northeast section near Pebble Creek, Willow Park near Indian Creek campground, and Swan Lake Flat. Less than 200 moose are found here, but just south of Yellowstone, Grand Teton National Park is prime moose habitat, and they are often spotted at Oxbow Lake.

PRONGHORN
Antilocapra americana
Pronghorn family (Antilocapridae)
Quick ID: reddish-brown; white on belly, sides, and throat; large white rump patch; males have black cheek patch; black horns on female not pronged, while those of males are pronged and about 10–16"
Length: 4.3–4.6' Weight: 75–140 lb

In the theater of wilderness, speed can mean survival or death. With lightning speed and agility, pronghorns can reach 45–50 mph, outrunning any major predator. As the sole surviving member of its family, the pronghorn was able to outrun and outlive the long-extinct American cheetah. This fastest land mammal in the Western Hemisphere once numbered in the millions on the North American plains. About 400 pronghorn can be found in and near the northern portion of Yellowstone and are especially easy to see near the North Entrance at Gardiner, Montana. In summer, pronghorn can be spotted in Lamar Valley along with great herds of bison. Visitors in June may be rewarded with views of tiny spotted twin pronghorns romping in the sagebrush-studded meadows.

BISON
Bison bison
Antelope, cattle, goat, and sheep family
(Bovidae)
Quick ID: huge; dark brown shaggy mane and beard;
hair longer in front than back; protruding shoulder
hump; huge head; black upward-curving horns
with pointed tips on male (bull) and female (cow);
up to 6' tall at shoulder; tail with tuft of hair at tip;
young (calf) reddish brown
Length: 7–12' Weight: 800–2,000 lb

An iconic symbol of the American west, millions of bison once ranged
freely from the Pacific coast to the Appalachians in the east. Since prehistoric times bison have roamed the Yellowstone ecosystem, but in the
1800s this magnificent species teetered on the brink of extinction. Successful conservation efforts in Yellowstone are evident now with about
4,900 bison grazing in Lamar, Hayden, Madison, Firehole, and Pelican
Valleys. The state mammal of Wyoming, bison congregate in Lamar and
Hayden Valleys in August during the rut or breeding season. Weighing
up to 1 ton, bulls clash in dust-clouded battles for the right to mate with
cows. These seemingly docile giants can race up to 32 mph and will
charge and gore anything, including humans, that get too close.

BIGHORN SHEEP
Ovis canadensis
Antelope, cattle, goat, and sheep family (Bovidae)
Quick ID: gray-brown coat; white rump patch, belly, and muzzle; about 3' tall at shoulder; male (ram) has large tan C-shaped curled horns that curve backward from forehead; horns of females (ewes) are smaller, shorter never reach a full curl
Length: 4'2"–6'1" Weight: 74–316 lb

The high meadows in and near Yellowstone are home to about 450 bighorn sheep that meander in 10–13 bands across the northern range. Most sheep migrate to lower elevations during winter and move to higher elevation ranges from May through October. One of the most reliable places in the park to see bighorns is on Mount Everts near the North Entrance at Gardiner, Montana. Agile climbers, bighorn sheep graze lush mountain meadows but find security from predators on rocky ledges. The massive horns of rams can curl up to 50 inches in length and weigh 40 pounds. Also found in the park, mountain goats, *Oreamnos americanus*, are similar in size and habitat use but are all white with sharp, pointed black horns.

MOUNTAIN GOAT
Oreamnos americanus
Antelope, cattle, goat, and sheep family (Bovidae)
Quick ID: long white fur (shed in summer); white chin beard in winter; sharp, backward-curving, 8–10" black horns
Length: 4'–5'10"   Weight: 150–300 lb

Fearless mountain climbers, the nimble-footed mountain goat effortlessly ascends to dizzying heights on tall mountaintops in Yellowstone. These nonnatives are descendants of mountain goats that were introduced for hunting purposes into Montana during the 1940s and 1950s. In and near the park, about 200–300 mountain goats compete with native bighorn sheep in similar alpine and subalpine habitats. You can identify mountain goats from a distance by their uniform whitish coats and black, pointed horns, whereas bighorns have a white rump patch, brownish-tan coats, and much larger, C-shaped, curved brownish horns. Bring your binoculars or spotting scope and try to spy mountain goats at Barronette Peak in the northeast section of the park.

CANADA GOOSE
Branta canadensis
Ducks, geese, and swans family (Anatidae)
Quick ID: long black neck; white cheeks (chinstrap); brown back; streaked tan breast
Length: 45" Weight: 9.8 lb Wingspan: 60"

In recent years, the Canada goose has increased its breeding range south from Canada and the northland and is now the familiar goose of parks and golf courses. Canada geese are currently being studied by ornithologists who now subdivide them into at least 11 subspecies based on size and other DNA characteristics. Typical of all Canada geese is the white cheek patch that extends below the chin (often called a chinstrap). They can be seen flying in the familiar V formation, proclaiming the recognizable "honk, honk" call. They prefer open areas where they can easily see any approaching predators. Canada geese can be seen throughout the park, including Hayden Valley, Old Faithful area, and Swan Lake Flat.

TRUMPETER SWAN
Cygnus buccinator
Ducks, geese, and swans family (Anatidae)
Quick ID: large; white; straight, black bill with reddish-pink border on lower bill; lacks any yellow on bill
Length: 60"   Weight: 23 lb   Wingspan: 80"

Known for its soulful, trumpetlike call, the trumpeter swan is the largest member of the waterfowl family in North America. Unfurling their long wings that can span up to 8 feet across, these magnificent birds once again ply the air over Yellowstone after their numbers dropped precipitously low in the 1920s due to habitat loss and overhunting. The other all-white, large bird in the park is the American pelican, *Pelecanus erythrorhynchos*, which has a heavy yellow bill and throat patch and black in the outer wings. Canada geese, *Branta canadensis*, have a black neck and gray body, and their neck is much shorter than that of the trumpeter swan in flight. To aid in the recovery process, park biologists are keeping a close watch on the swans in the park.

MALLARD
Anas platyrhynchos
Ducks, geese, and swans family (Anatidae)
Quick ID: male—green head; chestnut breast; white neck ring; yellow bill; female—brown; course markings; bill orange with dark splotch in center
Length: 23" Weight: 2.4 lb Wingspan: 35"

One of the most common and familiar species of duck in North America, the mallard easily adapts to human interferences. Male mallards have a yellow bill on a dark-green head bordered below by a thin white ring. Their brown chest and pale body ends with a characteristic curly tail. The female is dull brown with an orange bill. Found in many wetland habitats in the park, you can see mallards in many of the rivers and lakes in the park. In these same areas, look for other ducks, including gadwall, *A. strepera*; American wigeon, *A. americana*; northern shovelers, *A. clypeata*; northern pintails, *A. acuta*; and lesser scaup, *Aythya affinis*.

GREEN-WINGED TEAL
Anas crecca
Ducks, geese, and swans family
(Anatidae)
Quick ID: small duck; buffy stripe near tail;
green patch in wings (often concealed when swimming); male—dark rufous and thick
green "teal" stripe on head; brown back, gray body; female—mottled brown overall
Length: 14"   Weight: 12 oz   Wingspan: 23"

Green-winged teal are very small ducks with quick wing beats in flight.
Teals are dabbling, or puddle, ducks that generally search for food by
tipping their head down into the water. This behavior can help catego-
rize several other ducks in the park. The cinnamon teal, *A. cyanoptera*, is
larger with dark reddish-brown feathers on the male. American wigeon,
A. americana, males have a similar green facial stripe, but they have a
whitish stripe in the middle of their head, which the female lacks. Northern shovelers, *A. clypeata*, have a distinctive long spoon-shaped bill.
Gadwall, *A. strepera*, males are gray-brown with a black patch near the
tail. Northern pintails, *A. acuta*, have long necks, and the male has a long
pointed tail.

LESSER SCAUP
Aythya affinis
Ducks, geese, and swans family
(Anatidae)

Quick ID: medium-size duck; dark brownish; white patch at base of bill; yellow eye; male—black head, neck, chest, and rump; coarse barring on back; whitish sides; bluish bill with small black tip; female—dark brownish

Length: 16.5" Weight: 1.8 lb Wingspan: 25"

The lesser scaup is commonly seen on the waters of Yellowstone. The name *scaup* refers to shellfish beds, as these ducks like to eat crustaceans. This is one of the most widespread and abundant diving ducks in North America. Diving ducks are sometimes called bay or sea ducks, but many of them are commonly found on rivers, lakes, and ponds. These ducks tend to dive deep into the water to feed rather than simply tip their heads down like dabbling ducks.

The very similar male ring-necked duck, *A. collaris*, has a black back, gray sides, and white shoulder, while lesser scaups appear dark at both ends with gray in the middle. Male ring-necks also have a blue bill with a white ring and black tip.

HARLEQUIN DUCK
Histrionicus histrionicus
Ducks, geese, and swans family (Anatidae)
Quick ID: medium-size; male—bluish-gray back, neck, and head; black-bordered white markings on head and breast; chestnut brown on lower sides; female—brown; round white spot behind eye, white under eye
Length: 16.5" Weight: 1.3 lb Wingspan: 26"

The sight of a harlequin duck calmly perched on a rock in the midst of crashing whitewater rapids is an amazing thing to behold. These interesting ducks swim against the current, then dive underwater to forage for aquatic insects, mollusks, and crustaceans. Their densely packed feathers trap insulating air, making them very buoyant, and they seem to bounce out of the water and back onto the slippery rock perches. The male's striking patterns make it one of the most sought-after birds for nature watchers to see. The Latin name comes from the word *histrio*, which means "actor." Although not very common in Yellowstone, look for harlequins at LeHardy Rapids, Madison River, and Soda Butte Creek.

BARROW'S GOLDENEYE
Bucephala islandica
Ducks, geese, and swans family (Anatidae)
Quick ID: medium-size; short bill; head more flattened than rounded; yellow eye; male—black and white; purplish head; white crescent at base of bill; female—grayish-brown body; brown head; yellowish bill
Length: 18" Weight: 2.1 lb Wingspan: 28"

One of the most common ducks found in Yellowstone, Barrow's goldeneye is a bird of the western mountain regions of North America. Barrow's goldeneye was named to honor an English statesman, Sir John Barrow (1764–1848). The male Barrow's goldeneye is white with a black back and head. It has a distinctive white crescent between the eye and the bill. The very similar common goldeneye, *B. clangula*, can also be found in the park, especially in winter, but it has a rounded white spot in front of the eye, and its head is more peaked than the flattish head of the Barrow's. Both goldeneyes are smaller than mallards. Look for Barrow's goldeneye at Trout Lake, Yellowstone Lake, and Grant marina.

COMMON MERGANSER
Mergus merganser
Ducks, geese, and swans family (Anatidae)
Quick ID: male—greenish head; black back; white body; tapered orange-red bill;
female—chestnut head and throat; gray breast; white chin patch
Length: 25" Weight: 3.4 lb Wingspan: 34"

A duck with an unusual-looking bill, mergansers are characterized by a
long, narrow bill with serrations that help them grasp slippery fish. Common merganser males have a dark head and white body, while females
have a rusty-brown head and gray body; both have a slender orange
bill. Look for common mergansers on many lakes and rivers in the park,
including Mary Bay on Yellowstone Lake and LeHardy Rapids. Hooded
mergansers, *Lophodytes cucullatus*, and red-breasted mergansers, *M. ser-
rator*, may also be found in the park, but these are not as frequent.

Other ducks that you might see, especially in Hayden Valley, are ring-
necked ducks, *Aythya collaris*, and cinnamon teal, *Anas cyanoptera*.

RUDDY DUCK
Oxyura jamaicensis
Ducks, geese, and swans family (Anatidae)
Quick ID: small, compact duck; relatively large head; stiff tail often raised upright; male—black head; white cheek patch to bill; light blue bill; ruddy brown body; female—dark gray-brown; gray bill
Length: 15" Weight: 1.2 lb Wingspan: 18.5"

Many ducks make use of the abundant lakes, rivers, and streams in Yellowstone, but one that attracts visitor interest is the ruddy duck. This small duck has an unusual habit of sticking its tail straight up when swimming. The male also sports a stunning sky-blue bill in breeding season. Look for ruddy ducks at Blacktail Ponds and Floating Island. Another small duck with white on its head is the bufflehead, *Bucephala albeola*. Bufflehead males have a white patch leading in a triangle to the back of their head. They have bright white underparts that contrast with a blackish back. The female is dull brownish-gray with a small white cheek patch.

DUSKY GROUSE
Dendragapus obscurus
Upland game bird family (Phasianidae)
Quick ID: large, stocky, chicken-like bird; long neck and tail; gray-brown; feathers edged with tan and white mottling; grayish tail band; male—yellow "eyebrows"; red throat patches surrounded by white ring of feathers; female—paler; lacks yellow "eyebrows" and throat patches
Length: 20" Weight: 2.3 lb Wingspan: 26"

Bobbing its head and scratching the ground for seeds, the dusky grouse somewhat resembles a cross between a chicken and a turkey. When displaying, the male fans its tail and puffs out curious reddish air sacs surrounded by a circle of bright white feathers on either side of his neck. In forested areas, his low hoots sound a bit like air blowing across a bottle but it is often difficult to determine the origin of the sound. These grouse prefer grassy areas, where they forage for insects including grasshoppers, but they move into nearby forest for cover. Showing little fear of humans, the dusky grouse can sometimes be observed foraging along parking areas or roads such as Mount Washburn and Lake Butte Overlook.

COMMON LOON
Gavia immer
Loon family (Gaviidae)
Quick ID: black head; thin, dark neck; long, thin body checkered black and white; white breast; black bill is daggerlike
Length: 32" Weight: 9 lb Wingspan: 46"

For many people, the melancholy call of a loon floating across the waters of the northlands is one of the sounds of true wilderness. In the western United States, common loons breed in Idaho, Montana, Washington, and Wyoming, and the less than 30 loons that can be found in the park are some of the most southerly breeding populations in North America. Park biologists keep a careful watch on loons in the park. Listen and look for loons at Yellowstone Lake, Mary Bay, Lewis Lake, and Heart Lake. The double-crested cormorant, *Phalacrocorax auritus*, is another large diving bird that occurs in the park. The cormorant is all black with a longer neck and a hooked yellow bill.

EARED GREBE
Podiceps nigricollis
Grebe family (Podicipedidae)
Quick ID: small; duck-like; dark back; rusty sides; black neck and head; "fan" of wispy yellow cheek feathers; red eye; small, pointed, slightly upturned bill; long, thin neck; rump and tail sometimes look fluffy; gray and white in nonbreeding plumage
Length: 13" Weight: 11 oz Wingspan: 18"

As far as grebes go, the eared grebe is the most abundant member of the grebe family in the world. In Yellowstone, the far more commonly seen pied-billed grebe, *Podilymbus podiceps*, is brownish and smaller with a grayish-yellow bill and no facial markings. The thick, short yellowish-brown bill of the pied-bill grebe lightens to white during the breeding season and sports a black band. The pied-bill grebe is found throughout the park. However, it is the eared grebe that attracts much attention from visitors who chance upon this bird. Its startling blood-red eyes and golden plumes on its head conjure up tales of a demon duck-like bird swimming in the water. You may be able to spot the eared grebe at Fishing Bridge, Trout Lake, and Gull Point Drive.

AMERICAN WHITE PELICAN
Pelecanus erythrorhynchos
Pelican and cormorant family (Pelecanidae)
Quick ID: very large; white; outer wing feathers black; bill and large throat pouch yellow
Length: 50–65" Weight: 10–19.5 lb Wingspan: 108"

Often forming V-shaped squadrons, American white pelicans soar majes-
tically like avian hang gliders over Yellowstone Lake, surveying their
domain for schools of fish. Boasting a 9-foot wingspan and reaching a
height of 4 feet, the American white pelican is one of the largest birds
in North America. Pelicans use their large yellow, expandable pouch to
scoop up fish swimming in shallow waters. In breeding season, the adults
develop a fibrous plate on their bill like a small fin, which falls off after
mating season. Look for pelicans on Yellowstone Lake, the Yellowstone
and Madison Rivers, and at Fishing Bridge and Pelican Creek. The other
large white bird is the trumpeter swan, Cygnus buccinator, which lacks
the large throat pouch of the pelican and has pure white wings.

GREAT BLUE HERON
Ardea herodias
Heron and egret family (Ardeidae)
Quick ID: tall; gray; long legs; long neck; long, heavy pale yellow bill; two-toned wings in flight
Length: 46" Weight: 5.3 lb Wingspan: 72"

The great blue heron is the largest member of its family in North America. These large blue-gray herons are often mistaken for cranes or storks. "Great blues" fly with their necks curved into an S shape. Other large wetland birds such as sandhill cranes, *Grus canadensis*, trumpeter swans, *Cygnus buccinator*, and Canada geese, *Branta canadensis*, fly with their necks outstretched. Great blue herons are commonly found along rivers, lakes, and ponds and will eat fish, frogs, and even small mammals. In their graceful slow flight, they trail their long legs behind them, sometimes uttering a loud guttural "raaak" call. Nez Perce Ford picnic area is a great place to spot these large birds as well as many other waterbirds.

OSPREY
Pandion haliaetus
Osprey family (Pandionidae)
Quick ID: large; crooked wings; brown on top; white under body; dark mask across eyes, dark hooked bill; wings appear black-and-white checkered underneath; flies with wings crooked
Length: 23" Weight: 3.5 lb Wingspan: 63"

Osprey are large raptors commonly seen flying with crooked wings over rivers and lakes. Until DDT was banned in 1972, these birds and other large raptors were threatened to near extinction as a result of the pesticide thinning their eggshells. In full recovery now, osprey typically lay 2–4 eggs in a large stick nest. In Yellowstone, "fish hawks," as osprey are sometimes called, prefer dining on cutthroat trout; therefore, look for these large birds fishing in trout-inhabited rivers and streams. In a fascinating display, osprey often hover over the water, plunging down feet first to catch an unsuspecting fish. Listen for their sharp whistles in Lamar and Hayden Valleys, along the Gardner River in the Mammoth area, and at Inspiration Point.

BALD EAGLE
Haliaeetus leucocephalus
Diurnal raptor family (Accipitridae)
Quick ID: large raptor; brown body and wings; white head and tail as adult; yellow bill and feet; juveniles all brown or patchy brown and white with mottled brown head and tail
Length: 31" Weight: 9.5 lb Wingspan: 80"

For visitors who have never spotted a bald eagle in the wild, Yellowstone is a great place to tick this raptor off your list. Bald eagles are primarily fish eaters and, with an abundance of rivers and lakes, the park holds prime refuge for this magnificent bird. It takes a young bald eagle 4 years to molt into the recognizable white head and tail; therefore, other large birds such as turkey vultures, *Cathartes aura*, and osprey, *Pandion haliaetus*, may fool the eye. The golden eagle, *Aquila chrysaetos*, may dine along with the bald eagle at a carrion feast. Look for bald eagles along rivers including Yellowstone, Madison, Gardner, and Gibbon. You also have a good chance at spotting them at Lamar and Hayden Valleys, Slough Creek, and LeHardy Rapids.

SWAINSON'S HAWK
Buteo swainsoni
Diurnal raptor family (Accipitridae)
Quick ID: slender hawk; long wings; short tail; wings often held in shallow V shape when soaring; dark brown throat and chest; brown or gray upperparts; variable light, intermediate, or dark; male—gray head; female—brown head
Length: 19" Weight: 1.9 lb Wingspan: 51"

Buteos such as the Swainson's hawk have broad wings and relatively short tails. Named to honor the early 19th-century British naturalist William Swainson, these raptors winter in Argentina and return to the western states in spring. Look for Swainson's hawks at Fishing Bridge, Mount Washburn, Bridge Bay, and Nez Perce Ford picnic area. Other *buteos* found in Yellowstone include wintering rough-legged hawks, *B. lagopus*, and the very common red-tailed hawk, *B. jamaicensis*, which has a characteristic rusty-red tail. With relatively short rounded wings and long tails, accipiters such as Cooper's, *Accipiter cooperii*, and sharp-shinned hawks, *A. striatus*, are both much smaller than Swainson's hawk, but the northern goshawk, *A. gentilis*, is larger. Female northern harriers, *Circus cyaneus*, have vertical brown belly streaks, while males are pale gray on back.

90

RED-TAILED HAWK
Buteo jamaicensis
Diurnal raptor family (Accipitridae)
Quick ID: large brown hawk; broad, rounded wings; broad reddish tail; streaked belly-band; in flight, dark bar between shoulder and wrist is evident under wings
Length: 19" Weight: 2.4 lb Wingspan: 49"

Red-tailed hawks are one of the most common raptors seen in Yellowstone. These are often the first raptor learned by novice birders, as these hawks have a characteristic rusty-red tail and a darkly streaked bellyband. Young birds don't acquire the red tail until they are over 2 years old, and they have a gray-banded tail, which can cause some identification confusion. Red-tailed hawks are one of the most variable hawks, as some in the east are often paler than their western counterparts. Often seen soaring in broad circles and hunting for prey such as small rodents, look for redtails throughout the park but especially at Mount Washburn, Blacktail Plateau Drive, Swan Lake, Hayden Valley, Lamar Valley, and Mammoth.

GOLDEN EAGLE
Aquila chrysaetos
Diurnal raptor family (Accipitridae)
Quick ID: very large, dark-brown raptor, golden head, long wings; juveniles have white in tail and a white patch in wings
Length: 30" Weight: 10 lb Wingspan: 79"

North America's largest raptor, golden eagles are found where tall peaks dominate the landscape. Strong fliers, they nest on rocky ledges where they fledge 1 or 2 young in a season. Golden eagles take 3 years to reach adult plumage, and they often have a white patch near the end of their wings as well as a white band on the tail. When "goldens" fly, they hold their wings at in slight V, not unlike the smaller turkey vulture, *Cathartes aura*, which has a broad silvery sheen to the flight feathers. Goldens prey mainly on rabbits, marmots, and ground squirrels but will also eat carrion. Keep your eyes on the sky in Lamar and Hayden Valleys, and near Pebble Creek and Blacktail Plateau Drive.

AMERICAN COOT
Fulica americana
Rails, gallinules, and coots family (Rallidae)
Quick ID: round duck-like body; dusky black; cone-shaped, pointed white bill; red spot on forehead; greenish legs; lobed toes
Length: 15.5" Weight: 1.4 lb Wingspan: 24"

One of the easiest waterfowl for beginning birders to learn to identify, the American coot has a distinctive white bill set against an all-black body. Coots often share the same type of watery habitat with ducks, but they are actually more closely related to sandhill cranes and sora rails that lurk on the borders of ponds and wetlands. American coots have lobes of skin on their toes rather than the webbed feet of ducks. Commonly called "mud hens," they are rather clumsy walkers and require long running takeoffs to get airborne. The word *coot* is probably derived from the Latin word *fuligo*, which means "soot," in reference to the dusky black coloration. Look for coots on Slough Creek, Floating Island, and in Hayden Valley.

SANDHILL CRANE
Grus canadensis
Crane family (Gruidae)
Quick ID: large; pale silvery-gray; long dark-gray legs; red patch on crown; white patch on cheek; gray downward-curved rump feathers; may have rusty-orange on back
Length: 46" Weight: 10.6 lb Wingspan: 77"

So familiar is the tale of storks delivering babies that many people don't realize that other large birds with long legs and long necks even exist. One such bird is the sandhill crane that sometimes gathers in large flocks in the interior of North America. Arriving from their southern wintering grounds in early April, sandhill cranes nest in Yellowstone, raising one chick a year.

These cranes glide with their neck extended in flight and long, dark legs trailing behind. Other large birds in the park include the great blue heron, *Ardea herodias*, and rarely the white-faced ibis, *Plegadis chihi*. Look for sandhill cranes grazing in wet meadows at Floating Island Lake, Firehole Lake Drive, South Twin Lake, Blacktail Deer Plateau, and Tower Junction area.

AMERICAN AVOCET
Recurvirostra americana
Avocet and stilt family
(Recurvirostridae)

Quick ID: large shorebird; broad black and white stripes on back; long blue-gray legs and feet; long, thin upturned black bill; head buffy-red in summer, grayish-white in winter

Length: 18"   Weight: 11 oz   Wingspan: 31"

The American avocet is a large shorebird with distinctive black-and-white striping on its back and a peculiar thin, upturned bill. As they wade in shallow water, they sweep their long, thin bill side to side, searching for small crustaceans and insects. Although typically seen only in the park in spring and fall migration, their striking plumage attracts the attention of visitors. Avocets are sometimes confused with another large black-and-white wading bird, the black-necked stilt, *Himantopus mexicanus*, which has black on the top of its neck and head. Hayden Valley and Blacktail Ponds are good places to look for this and other wetland birds such as Wilson's phalaropes, *Phalaropus tricolor*. Also, watch for the long-billed curlew, *Numenius americanus*, which sports a very long 8-inch down-turned bill.

KILLDEER
Charadrius vociferous
Plover family (Charadriidae)
Quick ID: shorebird; light rusty-brownish back; white neck and belly; long rusty-orange tail with white-edged black tip; 2 prominent black chest bands; red eye ring; short black bill; long pointed wings, white wing stripe noticeable in flight
Length: 10.5" Weight: 3.3 oz Wingspan: 24"

To most people the ephydrid flies that live in the warm geyser waters are not the most appealing wildlife to watch, but for one shorebird, these flies are a buffet laid out for a feast. Killdeer can be seen in thermal and other open areas of the park snapping up ephydrid flies and other insects as they fretfully prance about on long spindly legs. The killdeer is so named for the loud "kil-deear dee-dee-dee" call that it makes. In an effort to distract predators from its chicks, an adult will pretend that it has a broken wing, calling loudly to lure the predator away. Look for killdeer at Specimen pond, Mammoth Terraces, Sand Point, and the geyser basins at Old Faithful.

SPOTTED SANDPIPER
Actitis macularius
Sandpiper family (Scolopacidae)
Quick ID: light-brown back and head; white underparts with bold dark spots; horizontal body bobs and teeters; white eye ring; white stripe over eye in breeding plumage; yellowish-orange bill with black tip; often bobs tail as it walks
Length: 7.5"   Weight: 1.4 oz   Wingspan: 15"

The constant bobbing and teetering of this shorebird is a good sign that you are looking at a spotted sandpiper. One of the easiest of the shorebirds to identify, this sandpiper has distinctive brown spots with a background of white on its throat and chest. It often walks holding its body in a horizontal position while bobbing its tail. Spotted sandpipers can be found in many areas of the park, including Grant Village marina, Phantom Lake, and Mammoth area, especially near the hot springs. Many other shorebirds may be seen enjoying insect feasts along the shores of the numerous lakes and rivers in the park on their annual migrations, including Baird's sandpiper, *Calidris bairdii*, and greater yellowlegs, *Tringa melanoleuca*.

CALIFORNIA GULL
Larus californicus
Gull and tern family (Laridae)
Quick ID: large gull; white head and underparts; gray back and wings; greenish-yellow legs; yellow bill with black and red mark near tip when in breeding plumage
Length: 21" Weight: 1.3 lb Wingspan: 54"

Two gulls that are commonly seen in Yellowstone are the California gull and the ring-billed gull, *L. delawarensis*. Smaller than California gulls and less frequent here, ring-billed gulls have a distinctive ring around their yellow bill. Closely related to gulls, terns including Caspian tern, *Hydroprogne caspia*, and common tern, *Sterna hirundo*, can also be found here. Terns have long pointed wings and dive headfirst to capture fish. The Caspian tern is the largest tern in the world and often makes a loud raspy "kowk" call in flight. The common tern is indeed the most common tern throughout North America. Look for gulls and terns near rivers and especially around Yellowstone Lake, including the marina at Grant Village, Bridge Bay, West Thumb, and Gull Point Drive.

GREAT GRAY OWL
Strix nebulosi
Owl family (Strigidae)
Quick ID: very large; mottled gray; rounded head without ear tufts; ring of concentric feathers surround each yellow eye; black and white "bow-tie" marking under face
Length: 27" Weight: 2.4 lb Wingspan: 52"

To the very observant or the very lucky, nothing arouses a sense of excitement more than hearing the deep baritone of a great gray owl calling in the night. As the largest owl in North America, great grays fly silently over meadows on broad wings approaching 60 inches across. They often nest in dead trees, called snags, where typically 2 or 3 young are hatched. In Yellowstone, great grays prey mainly on pocket gophers, locating them with keen hearing before pouncing even through deep snow. Great grays dwarf other smaller owls found in Yellowstone including northern saw-whet, *Aegolius acadicus*; boreal, *A. funereus*; and northern pygmy owls, *Glaucidium gnoma*. Great horned owls, *Bubo virginianus* (inset), are the most commonly seen owls and often nest in the Mammoth area.

WHITE-THROATED SWIFT
Aeronautes saxatalis
Swift family (Apodidae)
Quick ID: cylindrical body; long, narrow, pointed swept-back wings; black back, wings, and tail; white throat, belly, and sides; tail slightly forked; tiny feet
Length: 6.5" Weight: 1.1 oz Wingspan: 15"

Visitors to Yellowstone often stand in awe looking at the giant vertical basalt formations near Tower Fall. They soon notice tiny birds on stiff wings, soaring like jet-powered gliders, zipping around these vertical columns. Unlike most birds, white-throated swifts can flap their wings independently giving them the aerial agility to perform impressive aerial acrobatics in midair. The genus name, *Aeronautes*, is Greek for "sailor through the air." The species name, *saxatalis*, is derived from the Latin for "rock-inhabiting," as it nests on rocky cliffs. While the white-throated swift is the only swift found in the park, birds called swallows are also commonly seen. Six swallows can be found in the park, including violet-green, *Tachycineta thalassina*; tree, *T. bicolor*; cliff, *Petrochelidon pyrrho-nota*; and barn swallows, *Hirundo rustica*.

WILLIAMSON'S SAPSUCKER
Sphyrapicus thyroideus
Woodpecker family (Picidae)
Quick ID: medium-size woodpecker; yellowish belly; male—mostly black; white facial stripes, white rump; red chin patch; female—uniform brown bars, brown head
Length: 9" Weight: 1.8 oz Wingspan: 17"

Sapsuckers are a type of woodpecker that feeds by drilling holes in neat horizontal lines. Most male and female woodpeckers display similar plumages, but male and female (lower right) Williamson's sapsuckers are so unlike that they appear to be different species and were thought to be so until 1873. Williamson's sapsucker was named to honor Lt. Robert Stockton Williamson, a topographical engineer who took part in western surveying expeditions in the mid-1800s. The much larger and more commonly seen northern flicker, *Colaptes auratus* (upper right), has a brown back with black bars, gray head, and black spots on a whitish belly and red feather shafts visible in flight. Flickers can be seen throughout the park, but look for Williamson's sapsuckers especially at Calcite Springs Overlook and Blacktail Plateau Drive.

101

AMERICAN THREE-TOED WOODPECKER
Picoides tridactylus
Woodpecker family (Picidae)
Quick ID: medium-size black-and-white woodpecker; throat, breast, and belly white; back white with black edging; yellow spot on forehead
Length: 8.75" Weight: 2.3 oz Wingspan: 15"

The resounding rapid-fire hammering on a tree trunk is often the first clue that a woodpecker is nearby. Most woodpeckers have 2 toes forward and 2 toes backward, but the American three-toed woodpecker is missing one of the back toes. Similar in size and coloration to the more commonly seen hairy woodpecker, *P. villosus* (inset), the three-toed woodpecker has a yellow spot on its forehead rather than the red head spot of the hairy. Sightings of this woodpecker are often sought by birders. Look for the American three-toed woodpecker at Slough Creek, Firehole Lake Drive, Tower-Roosevelt, and Blacktail Plateau Drive. Also, look for these and other woodpeckers in burned areas of the park, including the area near the Petrified Tree display.

AMERICAN KESTREL
Falco sparverius
Falcon family (Falconidae)
Quick ID: small falcon; male—head with bold black stripes, contrasting with white cheeks, gray and tan on top and back of neck; rufous back with black horizontal stripes; blue-gray wings; female—lacks blue-gray and is mostly brown and rust
Length: 9" Weight: 4.1 oz Wingspan: 22"

One of the most frequently seen falcons, the American kestrel is the smallest of the trio of falcons that breed in the park. Both the prairie falcon, *F. mexicanus* (left inset), and the peregrine falcon, *F. peregrinus* (right inset), are much larger than the relatively small kestrel. Another uncommon falcon visitor is the merlin, *F. columbarius*. Kestrels have a habit of sitting on overhead wires, poles, or branches while they survey the surrounding ground for insects or small rodents. They have the ability to hover in one spot before swiftly plunging down to strike. Kestrels are sometimes called "sparrow hawks" in reference to their small size. You can find kestrels throughout the park, but they are especially abundant in Mammoth, Lamar Valley, and the Canyon area.

GRAY JAY
Perisoreus canadensis
Crow and jay family (Corvidae)
Quick ID: dark gray above; pale gray below; whitish forehead with dark cap; whitish throat; short black bill
Length: 11.5" Weight: 2.5 oz Wingspan: 18"

Jays and other members of the family Corvidae are among the most intelligent birds, and along with the Clark's nutcracker, *Nucifraga columbiana*, and Steller's jay, *Cyanocitta stelleri*, the gray jay has earned the nickname "camp robber" from the practice of stealing food from unattended picnic tables or camps. The larger Clark's nutcrackers have black wings and a long black bill, while Steller's jays are all blue with a crest on their head. Gray jays spend the summer gathering and storing food for the winter. Using the unusually sticky saliva that they produce, they glue small blobs of gathered food items under bark or lichens or in the forks of trees. These numerous caches of solidified seeds, insects, and fungi are important for their winter survival.

STELLER'S JAY
Cyanocitta stelleri
Crow and jay family (Corvidae)
Quick ID: azure blue body, wings, and tail; head, breast, and back blackish; long bluish-black crest on head
Length: 11.5" Weight: 3.7 oz Wingspan: 19"

The tall, pointed head crest and azure blue feathers of the Steller's jay make it one of the easiest birds to identify. Its eastern counterpart, the blue jay, *C. cristata*, is the only other jay with a crest, but it has white facial markings rather than the black markings of the Steller's jay. Fearless and smart, the Steller's jay's keen eye for an easy meal has earned it the dubious nickname "camp robber." Another jay called the pinyon jay, *Gymnorhinus cyanocephalus*, can be found near the North Entrance near Gardiner, Montana. Often traveling in small flocks, this raucous bird is dusty blue-gray with a whitish throat, and it lacks the crest of the Steller's jay. Pinyon jays superficially resemble mountain bluebirds, but Pinyon jays are much larger and paler gray-blue.

CLARK'S NUTCRACKER
Nucifraga columbiana
Crow and jay family (Corvidae)
Quick ID: pale gray; black wings with white patches; pointed black bill; black tail with white outer tail feathers
Length: 12" Weight: 4.6 oz Wingspan: 24"

Some visitors to Yellowstone have remarked that Clark's nutcrackers look like baby bald eagles. Although quite bold and brave, they are more closely related to crows and ravens than eagles. These daring birds frequent picnic areas, totally unaware of signs that warn visitors not to feed the animals. Named for William Clark of the famed Lewis and Clark Expedition, Clark's nutcracker uses its long sharp bill to open conifer cones to feed on the nutritious seeds. It also has a special pouch under its tongue in which it can hold many seeds. Masters at storing food, these birds hide seeds in hundreds of caches for later use. Look for Clark's nutcrackers at Mount Washburn, Mammoth, and picnic areas such as those at Fishing Bridge.

BLACK-BILLED MAGPIE
Pica hudsonia
Crow and jay family (Corvidae)
Quick ID: large; black; white patch on shoulder; white belly; very long tail; iridescent green and blue on wings and tail; swaggering walk
Length: 19" Weight: 6 oz Wingspan: 25"

Not likely to be confused with any other bird, the striking tuxedo look that the black-billed magpie proudly shows off is well recognized across the western states, but this large crow-size bird is often a novelty for visitors from the east. The conspicuously long, iridescent tail makes up half the total length of the bird. Magpies are intelligent and resourceful birds. They have been known to sit on the backs of elk and other large ungulates to glean insects for an easy meal. Black-billed magpies are year-round residents of Yellowstone National Park and can be predictably found around the parking areas and campground in Mammoth. They are one of the most commonly seen birds on the annual winter Christmas Bird Count.

COMMON RAVEN
Corvus corax
Crow and jay family (Corvidae)
Quick ID: large; solid black; long narrow wings; wedge-shaped tail; heavy black bill
Length: 24" Weight: 2.6 lb Wingspan: 53"

Noted for their ability to solve complex cause-and-effect problems, ravens have been the object of many scientific studies of intelligence. Their keen observation talents and advanced intellectual capabilities place ravens in a category with other highly advanced predators. In a unique symbiotic relationship, ravens act as scouts for wolves, leading them to carcasses by fluttering up and down. The ravens are able to scavenge the small scraps from the wolves' meal. Ravens have been observed playing with young wolf pups, creating a lasting bond of trust between the two; having observed this interaction, American Indians called ravens "wolf birds." In winter, especially, visitors are sometimes surprised to find their belongings have been taken by these tricksters.

CLIFF SWALLOW
Petrochelidon pyrrhonota
Swallow family (Hirundinidae)
Quick ID: pointed wings; small head with dark cap, square tail; dark gray above, pale below; chestnut-brown throat; whitish forehead; tawny rump
Length: 5.5" Weight: 0.74 oz Wingspan: 13.5"

Flocks of swallows often amass in huge swarms, jetting across the sky, snatching up vast numbers of insects in midair. The genus name for the cliff swallow, *Petrochelidon*, is Greek for "rock swallow," in reference to their natural nesting site on cliffs and overhangs; cliff swallows also take advantage of sheltered buildings to construct their mud nests. If you look carefully, many buildings and bridges in the park are adorned with mud nests. Tree swallows, *Tachycineta bicolor* (inset), which are also very common in the park, have glossy blue-green upperparts and snowy white underparts. Violet-green swallows, *T. thalassina*, have emerald-green backs and white on the face. Barn swallows, *Hirundo rustica*, have long deeply forked tails.

MOUNTAIN CHICKADEE
Poecile gambeli
Chickadee and titmice family
(Paridae)
Quick ID: gray back; buffy-white
underparts; gray wings; black cap;
white cheeks; black chin; white eyebrow; black line through eye
Length: 5.25" Weight: 0.39 oz Wingspan: 8.5"

You will probably hear the high-pitched, lively "chick-a-dee-dee" and "fee-bee" calls of the mountain chickadee before you see this tiny black-and-white bird. The mountain chickadee has a distinguishing white feathered eyebrow that helps to separate it from its relative, the black-capped chickadee, *P. atricapillus* (inset), which is less common in Yellowstone. Chickadees sometimes cling acrobatically to twigs or conifer cones as they forage for insects. In autumn, they busily cache conifer seeds for the winter ahead. When you find mountain chickadees, keep an eye out for other small birds, including red-breasted nuthatches, *Sitta canadensis*; brown creepers, *Certhia americana*; and ruby-crowned kinglets, *Regulus calendula*. Look for mountain chickadees throughout the park, including Mammoth campground, Roosevelt Lodge, Mount Washburn, and Yellowstone Lake.

AMERICAN DIPPER
Cinclus mexicanus
Dipper family (Cinclidae)
Quick ID: stocky gray body; relatively long legs; short tail, often cocked; short, pointed wings; often bobs up and down on streamside rocks
Length: 7.5" Weight: 2 oz Wingspan: 11"

The polar plunge antics of this small gray songbird make it one of the most interesting birds to watch in the wild. Also commonly known as water ouzel (pronounced OO-zuhl), the American dipper is a favorite of many nature lovers, including John Muir and President Theodore Roosevelt.

Living in Yellowstone throughout the year, dippers are distantly related to warblers and thrushes. Dippers have a unique method of searching for aquatic insects and other food by diving headfirst under the water, then walking or even swimming upstream underwater. These fascinating birds build dome-shaped nests in riverbanks and sometimes under bridges. Look for American dippers bobbing on rocks in fast-moving streams and rivers such as Lewis Falls, Lava Creek, Gardner River, and LeHardy Rapids.

RUBY-CROWNED KINGLET
Regulus calendula
Kinglet family (Regulidae)
Quick ID: tiny; olive-greenish-gray overall; white eye ring; black bill; short, rounded wings; darker wing and tail with yellow and white edging; male—red crown (not apparent all the time); female—olive-greenish-gray crown
Length: 4.25" Weight: 0.23 oz Wingspan: 7.5"

Ruby-crowned kinglets are tiny hyperactive birds constantly on the move, flicking their wings as they glean insects from tree branches. Male ruby-crowned kinglets have hidden ruby-red head feathers that they display when agitated. Smaller than warblers or chickadees and weighing only about as much as a quarter, you may hear the high-pitched staccato "zee-zee-zee" scolding before you see these tiny birds. In late April or early May, "ruby-crowns" arrive back to Yellowstone, where they breed in spruce and fir forests in the park. Look for kinglets in many areas of the park, including Lava Creek picnic area, Riverside Drive, and Trout Lake.

MOUNTAIN BLUEBIRD
Sialia currucoides
Thrush family (Turdidae)
Quick ID: thin, dark bill; long wings; black legs and feet; male—azure blue; female—pale brownish-gray with blue-tinged wings and tail
Length: 7.25" Weight: 1 oz Wingspan: 14"

After spending the cold winter months in the south, mountain bluebirds return to Yellowstone National Park in spring to breed and raise their brood. Renowned hunters, these small, alert birds often hover above their insect prey in a movement birders call "hawking." They often perch on exposed limbs overlooking open meadows, and, when an insect is spotted, they swoop down to grab it with their bills. Honored as the official state bird of Idaho, the males are brilliant, bright blue on top and sky blue on the belly. The female mountain bluebird is dull, pale bluish-gray, which may offer her camouflage protection while nesting. Look for these blue jewels near Old Faithful trails, Slough Creek, West Thumb Geyser Basin, Roosevelt area, and Blacktail Plateau Drive.

113

TOWNSEND'S SOLITAIRE
Myadestes townsendi
Thrush family (Turdidae)
Quick ID: long, slim, plain gray overall; white eye ring; white outer tail feathers; buffy wing patches
Length: 8.5" Weight: 1.2 oz Wingspan: 14.5"

One of the most commonly seen birds on the annual Christmas Bird Count is the Townsend's solitaire. A rather plain-looking gray bird, Townsend's solitaire is in the same family as American robins, *Turdus migratorius*. Somewhat resembling large, dark-eyed juncos, *Junco hyemalis*, both of these species have white outer tail feathers. The famous ornithologist John James Audubon named this bird to honor John Kirk Townsend, who first described the species in 1838. Townsend's solitaires feed on the blue berrylike fleshy cones of woody plants called Rocky Mountain junipers, *Juniperus scopulorum*. To find Townsend's solitaire look first for the junipers, and you will often see them perched on top, singing a sweet song. Junipers grow in the Mammoth campground and along the Upper Terrace Drive.

AMERICAN ROBIN
Turdus migratorius
Thrush family (Turdidae)
Quick ID: Upperparts gray to black; breast and underparts reddish-orange; broken white eye ring; yellow bill
Length: 10"   Weight: 2.7 oz   Wingspan: 17"

The American robin is one of the most widespread and familiar of all North American birds. A member of the thrush family, the American robin is named for an unrelated bird called the European robin that is similar in coloration. Robins are often seen hopping about on lawns, pulling at earthworms, or foraging for fruit and insects in shrubbery. While nesting and raising their chicks, these normally gentle birds will often dive-bomb predators in an effort to protect their offspring. When the brown-spotted chicks fledge, they remain on the ground or under cover in bushes or trees, often fluttering their wings and begging for food from their parents. The parents will often move away from them to avoid detection from predators.

YELLOW-RUMPED WARBLER
Setophaga coronata
Wood warbler family (Parulidae)
Quick ID: large warbler; white spots in tail; male—gray back with black markings; bright yellow throat, rump, and sides; white wing patch; blackish streaks on white sides; black on chest; female—brownish gray; yellow throat, rump, and sides
Length: 5.5" Weight: 0.43 oz Wingspan: 9.25"

Of the 50-plus species of warblers that can be found in North America, only a handful can be regularly seen in Yellowstone. Warblers are small songbirds that eat a wide variety of insects, fruits, and berries. The yellow-rumped warbler has two distinct subspecies. The somewhat duller "myrtle" warbler inhabits eastern North America, and the brighter "Audubon's" warbler is found in the west. You can see "yellow-rumps" in many areas of the park, including Slough Creek, Pebble Creek Campground, Grant Village, Lake Lodge, and Trout Lake. Observant nature lovers commonly see bright yellow warblers, *S. petechia*, and wetland-loving common yellowthroats, *Geothlypis trichas*. You may have to search a bit harder to find Wilson's warblers, *Cardellina pusilla*; and MacGillivray's warblers, *G. tolmiei*.

116

WHITE-CROWNED SPARROW
Zonotrichia leucophrys
Sparrow family (Emberizidae)
Quick ID: bold black and white stripes on cap; unstreaked grayish breast; brown-streaked back; pinkish to yellow bill; immature has rusty crown
Length: 7" Weight: 1.0 oz Wingspan: 9.5"

Sparrows are small brown-striped birds that tend to forage close to shrubby areas where they can dash for protection. Even for good birders, sparrows are often notoriously difficult to identify, but several, including the white-crowned sparrow, are easy to identify once you start noticing subtle variations and details. The white-crowned sparrow is easily recognized by the clean white and black stripes on its cap. Chipping sparrows, *S. passerina* (inset), are quite small and have a clear gray breast and a rusty cap. Song sparrows, *Melospiza melodia*, have a streaked breast, and Brewer's sparrows, *Spizella breweri*, are very subtly marked. Look for white-crowned sparrows and other sparrows at Soda Butte picnic area, Riverside Drive, Slough Creek, Mary Bay picnic area, Fishing Bridge, and Lake Butte Overlook.

DARK-EYED JUNCO
Junco hyemalis
Sparrow family (Emberizidae)
Quick ID: gray to brown to blackish above; white belly; variable pinkish sides; white outer tail feathers; feed on ground by hopping
Length: 6.25" Weight: 0.67 oz Wingspan: 9.25"

One of the most commonly seen small birds in Yellowstone is the dark-eyed junco. Much like the larger American robin, *Turdus migratorius*, as they feed on insects or seeds, dark-eyed juncos tend to hop or walk on the ground. Several subspecies can be found in Yellowstone, but the most common is the pink-sided junco, *J. h. mearnsi*. The Latin name originates from a 1747 book titled *Birds of Colonial America* by Mark Catesby, when he referred to the junco as a "snow bird." *Junco* is Latin for "rush," probably referring to similar European birds that live in reeds; *hyemalis* means "winter." Look for juncos in wooded areas at LeHardy Rapids, Riverside Drive, Norris Geyser Basin, and Tower Fall.

WESTERN TANAGER
Piranga ludoviciana
Cardinal family (Cardinalidae)
Quick ID: male—yellow body; black back, wings, and tail; orange-red head; female—greenish-yellow body and head; grayish back and wings
Length: 7.25" Weight: 0.98 oz Wingspan: 11.5"

It is the sight of a bird such as the western tanager that entices and intrigues some people to become avid birders. The bright poppy-red-and-orange head and neck, yellow body, and black back and wings of this bird definitely attract attention. Only the male western tanager is so colorful, as the female is dull yellow with a gray-brown back and yellow wing bars, which offer her camouflage protection at the nest. Previously placed in the tanager family, western tanagers have been recently moved to the cardinal family. Western tanagers migrate to Mexico and Costa Rica for the winter. Look for these lovely birds in many areas of the park, including the Old Faithful area, Boiling River trail, and Riverside Drive.

LAZULI BUNTING
Passerina amoena
Cardinal family (Cardinalidae)
Quick ID: stocky; short tail; short conical bill; male—bright sky-blue head and back, reddish-orange chest band, white belly; 2 white wing bars on dark wings; female—grayish brown above; dull brown below; dull tan wing bars
Length: 5.5" Weight: 0.54 oz Wingspan: 8.75"

With its eye-catching azure-blue head and back, the male lazuli bunting is easily recognized as it flits about in shrubby areas hunting for insects. The female is not as easy to spy, as her dull gray-brown coloration blends well with the surroundings. Named for the gemstone lapis lazuli, this bunting of western states sweetly sings from open perches on tall shrubs and branches. Visitors from the east may be familiar with the counterpart: the all-blue male indigo bunting, *P. cyanea*. The lazuli bunting may be confused with other blue birds in Yellowstone, including the mountain bluebird, *Sialia currucoides*, which is entirely blue with a narrow, pointed bill, and the Steller's jay, *Cyanocitta stelleri*, which is much larger with a crest on its head.

YELLOW-HEADED BLACKBIRD
Xanthocephalus xanthocephalus
Blackbird family (Icteridae)
Quick ID: male—black body; golden-yellow head, neck, and throat; fan-shaped all-black tail; black mask over eyes; white wing patch; female—mottled brown; dull yellow head, neck, and throat; white streaking on breast
Length: 9.5" Weight: 2.3 oz Wingspan: 15"

Although the conspicuous yellow and black plumage of the male is striking, it is often the loud raspy calls and chattering in wetlands that first attracts your attention to the yellow-headed blackbird. Red-winged blackbirds, *Agelaius phoeniceus*, are smaller than yellow-headed black-birds, and males lack the yellow head and sport wing red patches. Female "redwings" are streaky brown like the yellow-headed female but have less yellow in the face and throat. Yellow-headed blackbird males are polygynous, which means that males have as many as 8 female mates. The official state bird of both Wyoming and Montana, the western mead-owlark, *Sturnella neglecta*, also has yellow and black markings, but it has brownish streaking on the back. Listen and then look for yellow-headed blackbirds at Blacktail Ponds, Slough Creek, Nez Perce Ford picnic area, and Floating Island Lake.

121

BREWER'S BLACKBIRD
Euphagus cyanocephalus
Blackbird family (Icteridae)
Quick ID: male—dark, glossy purplish-green; female—gray-brown
Length: 9" Weight: 2.2 oz Wingspan: 15.5"

The dark plumage of a male Brewer's blackbird reflects bright sheens of purple and green. Females are dull brown with grayish overtones, which is an important feature for camouflage from predators while nesting. Brewer's blackbirds respond rapidly to insect outbreaks, capturing as many as 5 large insects per minute. In 1829, John James Audubon named this bird after Thomas Mayo Brewer, an ornithologist friend from Boston. Another blackbird found in the park is the red-winged blackbird, *Agelaius phoeniceus*; these "redwings" are easy to identify as the solid black feathers are accentuated by scarlet red and yellow shoulder patches. In wetlands, redwing males loudly proclaim their territory with a repeated "ko-ka-ree" call, while the brown-striped females tend their nests.

BROWN-HEADED COWBIRD
Molothrus ater
Blackbird family (Icteridae)
Quick ID: stout, conical bill; relatively short tail;
male—brown head, body black with greenish
gloss; female—dark brown, pale brown
streaked below
Length: 7.5" Weight: 1.5 oz Wingspan: 12"

Brown-headed cowbirds are often seen perched on the back of bison, picking insects off their shaggy coats. Female cowbirds somewhat resemble large female Cassin's finches, *Carpodacus cassinii*, but cowbirds are chunkier. In a behavior called nest parasitism, cowbirds lay their eggs in the nests of other birds, leaving the new host parents to care for their young. Look for brown-headed cowbirds anywhere bison are found, including Hayden Valley, Lamar Valley, Roosevelt area, Madison, and Gibbon Meadows. Brewer's blackbirds, *Euphagus cyanocephalus*, share the same habitat, but their bills are thinner, and they have yellow eyes. Often seen singing in these open meadows, the larger western meadowlarks, *Sturnella neglecta*, have a pointed bill and are yellowish with black and tan mottling.

GRAY-CROWNED ROSY-FINCH
Leucosticte tephrocotis
Finch family (Fringillidae)
Quick ID: streaked brown; head mostly gray with dark forehead; rosy feather patches on wings and sides
Length: 6.25" Weight: 0.91 oz Wingspan: 13"

Rosy-finches are one of the most sought-after sightings for avid birders. These small songbirds spend their lives in the high altitudes of western North America. Both the gray-crowned and black rosy-finch, *L. atrata* (inset), can be found in Yellowstone. Though not as commonly seen in the park, black rosy-finches have black on the head, back, and breast. Rosy-finches usually travel in small to large flocks, and sometimes are seen foraging for insects at the edges of melting snowfields. In winter, they eat seeds from grasses, sedges, and dried flower heads. In deep snow cover, they migrate to lower elevations and sometimes come to feeders set up outside park boundaries. Look for these birds in the alpine areas, including Mount Washburn, and along high-elevation areas of the park.

BLOTCHED TIGER SALAMANDER
Ambystoma tigrinum
Mole salamander family (Ambystomatidae)
Quick ID: thick neck and body; variable light-olive to black; yellow splotches on back and sides; broad head; wide mouth; large eyes; long tail
Length: 6.7–12.9"

The only salamander found in Yellowstone is the blotched tiger salamander. This large salamander is typically about 9 inches long, including its long tail. They are rarely seen in the open as they live in deep burrows or under logs or rocks. The aquatic larvae have external gills and a long caudal fin. Some adults may retain their external gills from the aquatic larval form their entire lives. The larvae are sometimes called waterdogs and outside the park are sometimes used as fishing bait, which is an unwise practice as these salamanders can transmit viruses and a fungal disease that can infect reptiles, amphibians, and fish. The spring migration to breeding ponds occurs in late April to June, especially in Lamar Valley after rain.

BOREAL TOAD
Bufo boreas boreas
True toad family (Bufonidae)
Quick ID: stocky; blunt nose; variable brown, gray, or olive-green; irregular black spots; dry, warty skin; creamy white stripe on back; oval parotid glands
Length: 3–5"

The boreal toad is the only toad found in Yellowstone. Boreal toads prefer wet habitats at high altitudes and are found in Colorado, Idaho, Washington, Utah, and Wyoming. Their numbers have been in decline because of a fungus that causes a skin disease in many species of amphibians. Instead of hopping like most frogs, boreal toads prefer to walk. They eat various invertebrates, such as worms, beetles, and spiders, with the aid of their long, sticky tongue. They will also eat algae and carrion. Boreal toads hibernate in underground burrows in the winter. In the park, they are preyed on by garter snakes, mammals, and large birds, including wading birds and ravens.

BOREAL CHORUS FROG
Pseudacris maculata
Tree frog family (Hylidae)
Quick ID: small frog; short legs; 3 dark bands on back; variable pale-gray to brown or green; dark line from snout to groin
Length: 1–1.5"

Not much larger than the diameter of a quarter, chorus frogs are tiny frogs that have a very loud voice. In spring, their "preep" call sounds like a thumbnail being run along a fine-toothed comb. They lay eggs in a mass attached to submerged vegetation in quiet water and hatch in about 2 weeks. The tadpoles metamorphose for about 2 months during summer. Fish, birds, mammals, and garter snakes eat the adults and tadpoles. In the evening, listen for these small frogs calling near Mud Volcano. The other frog that is commonly seen in the park is the Columbia spotted frog, *Rana luteiventris*. It is larger than the chorus frog but only reaches a bit over 3 inches.

SAGEBRUSH LIZARD
Sceloporus graciosus
Spiny lizard family (Phrynosomatidae)
Quick ID: keeled, spiny scales on back; grayish–pale brown; brown and tan stripes on back and sides; cream belly; males—blue patch on belly and throat
Length: 4.5–5"

The only lizard in Yellowstone, the sagebrush lizard is most commonly found in sagebrush areas near the North Entrance. It can also be seen in warm geyser basins such as Norris Geyser Basins and near Shoshone and Heart Lakes. Sagebrush lizards eat a variety of insects, such as ants, moths, and beetles, but quickly run for shelter if disturbed. They hibernate during the winter in old rodent burrows or other sheltered sites. Males have a unique way of fending off potential rivals: They raise their heads and do push-ups on rocks or other perch to show off the bright blue belly blotches. Sagebrush lizards are preyed upon by snakes and some birds.

BULL SNAKE
Pituophis catenifer sayi
Colubrid family (Colubridae)
Quick ID: yellowish; brown, black, or reddish-brown blotches on the back; blotchy rings around end of tail
Length: 50–72"

Although bull snakes look dangerous and sometimes act dangerous, they are nonvenomous. The bull snake found in Yellowstone in the Mammoth area is a subspecies of the gopher snake, of which there are 6 currently recognized subspecies. These snakes are helpful for keeping populations of rodents in check. When threatened by a predator, the bull snake can puff its body, curl into the recognizable strike position of a rattlesnake, and shake its rattleless tail. It is for this reason that bull snakes are often mistaken for the venomous prairie rattlesnake, *Crotalis viridis*, which is also found in the northern section of the park.

WANDERING GARTER SNAKE
Thamnophis elegans vagrans
Colubrid family (Colubridae)
Quick ID: variable brown, brownish-green, or gray; 3 light stripes with 1 center stripe the length of the body
Length: 6–30"

Though it is rarely seen, the wandering garter snake is the most common reptile in Yellowstone. It is one of 6 subspecies of the western terrestrial garter snake found throughout the west. They were called "wandering" because of the erroneous thought that they wander farther from water than other garter snakes. This harmless snake is typically found near water in areas with cover, such as Sheepeater Cliff. They are not fussy eaters and will take a variety of food including worms, small fish, and mice. Considered nonvenomous, recent studies have found they contain mild glandular proteins to help them digest their prey. The nearly black valley garter snake, *T. sirtalis fitchi*, is found only in the Bechler region of the park.

PRAIRIE RATTLESNAKE
Crotalus viridis
Pit viper family (Viperidae)
Quick ID: varied green, gray, light brown, or yellowish with dark brown splotches on the back that are bordered with a white ring; rattle on tail; triangular head; vertical pupils
Length: 35–48"

The only venomous snake in Yellowstone is the prairie rattlesnake. Although it can reach over 48 inches in length, they are not commonly seen as they are only found in a few drier and warmer areas in the northwest corner of the park. Rattlesnakes use venom to subdue their prey, which includes rodents, ground nesting birds, insects, and other invertebrates. The venom also begins the digestive process as it continues to break down proteins, which is one of the reasons that prairie rattlesnakes can survive Yellowstone's cold winter conditions that can slow digestion. Using the sensory organs in two pits under their nostrils that detect heat, they can hunt in complete darkness.

BROOK TROUT
Salvelinus fontinalis
Trout family (Salmonidae)
Quick ID: dark olive-green to brown; cream wavy lines (vermiculations) on back and head; sides with pale spots and red spots with bluish halos; bottom fins white-edged offset by black
Length: 5–9.8" Weight: 2.2–13.2 lb

Every year thousands of people visiting Yellowstone come for the joy of fishing the multitude of pristine waters. Even though many anglers have their eyes set on cutthroats, they can enjoy several other trout species. Pulling in a "brookie" is a delight for anglers of all experience levels.

Brook trout thrive in clean, cold streams with sufficient dissolved oxygen. Other game fish in the park are native Arctic grayling, *Thymallus arcticus*, and mountain whitefish, *Prosopium williamsoni*. Only lead-free barbless hooks and artificial lures or flies may be used in Yellowstone. Some streams or lakes are for fly fishing only and have specific posted regulations. Make sure to ask at one of the park visitor centers for fishing regulations or see the official Yellowstone National Park website at nps.gov/yell/planyourvisit/fishing.htm.

BROWN TROUT
Salmo trutta
Trout family (Salmonidae)
Quick ID: brown to gold; black spots, red spots with blue halos, unspotted tail
Length: 10–16" Weight: 1–20+ lb

Native to Europe, brown trout, or "brownies" as they are commonly called, were introduced into the west for sportfishing. These voracious predators compete with other fish, and declines of native trout species are common where these fish are found. Brown trout have been introduced into the Gardner and Yellowstone River systems. Secretive, they favor areas with overhanging vegetation, undercut banks, and submerged snags and rocks. Smaller brown trout feed on mayflies, caddisflies, and midges, while larger trout are predators of other fish, including other trout. Brown trout are wary and can be a challenging catch for anglers. Make sure to check with a local fly shop to see what insects are currently hatching.

LAKE TROUT
Salvelinus namaycush
Trout family (Salmonidae)
Quick ID: dark greenish with light-colored spots; deeply forked tail
Length: 14–20" Weight: 15–40 lb

The normally cold waters of Yellowstone are the natural home of native cutthroat that had thrived here until the illegal introduction of predatory lake trout in the 1980s. Lake trout or mackinaw are native in Canada and the Great Lakes and inhabit large, deep, cold lakes rather than rivers and streams. The lake trout are responsible for a severe reduction in the population of native cutthroat trout. The native cutthroats play a major role in the food web in the park, with over 40 species of animals that rely on them as a food source. Efforts are being made to reduce the population of lake trout so that the numbers of cutthroat can recover.

RAINBOW TROUT
Oncorhynchus mykiss
Trout family (Salmonidae)
Quick ID: small, uniform black spots; pinkish stripe on sides and cheeks; white tips on fins
Length: 12–18" Weight: 1–3 lb

Native to the Pacific coast, rainbow trout have been widely introduced into streams and rivers throughout North America, including those of Yellowstone. Rainbows were not native to Yellowstone but were introduced in the late 19th century. The rainbow trout has dense black specks on its body and most fins, and its tail is heavily spotted. The colorful pinkish stripe on its sides and cheeks give rise to the name rainbow trout. Rainbow trout are commonly found in the park, where cool, fast-flowing water is abundant in the many rivers and streams. A Yellowstone National Park fishing permit is required to fish in the park. Fishing permits can be obtained at visitor center, ranger stations, Yellowstone Park general stores, and at many businesses outside the park.

YELLOWSTONE CUTTHROAT TROUT
Oncorhynchus clarkii bouvieri
Trout family (Salmonidae)
Quick ID: color variable but generally yellowish-brown or brassy-bronzy; belly paler; medium-size round spots concentrated toward caudal fin (tail); red slash under lower jaw
Length: 7.8–15.7" Weight: 4.4–8.8 lb

Even though Yellowstone is well known as a great fishing park, the only native trout is the cutthroat trout, which is the official state fish of Idaho, Wyoming, and Montana. There are 2 subspecies: the Yellowstone cutthroat and the westslope cutthroat. The common name "cutthroat" refers to the red slash on the lower jaw that appears to be a wound. The species name, *clarkii*, honors William Clark of the famous Lewis and Clark Expedition. Cutthroat trout are an important source of food for grizzly bears in the park. The introduced lake trout in Yellowstone Lake are predatory on cutthroat and caused a significant decline in the population. Measures are under way to reduce the number of lake trout in the park.

ROCKY MOUNTAIN PARNASSIAN

Parnassius smintheus
Parnassian and swallowtail
family (Papilionidae)
Quick ID: relatively large; white with blackish-gray markings; red spots ringed with black
Wingspan: 1.7–2.5" Flight Season: June–August

Members of the swallowtail family of butterflies are large and usually have "tails" on their hind wings, such as those of the western tiger swallowtail. Even though the parnassians are members of the swallowtail family, they are all tailless. Rocky Mountain parnassians are fairly large white butterflies with black and red spots. They nectar on the flowers of asters and sedums.

WESTERN TIGER SWALLOWTAIL

Papilio rutulus
Parnassian and swallowtail
family (Papilionidae)
Quick ID: large; yellow with black stripes; 1 tail on each hind wing
Wingspan: 2.75–4"
Flight Season: June–July

One of the most familiar butterflies, the western tiger swallowtail delights butterfly lovers throughout most western states. The very similar two-tailed swallowtail, *P. multicaudata*, has narrower tiger stripes and 2 hair-like tails. Anise swallowtail, *P. zelicaon*, also has only 1 tail on each hind wing, but it has 2 orange eyespots.

SHERIDAN'S GREEN HAIRSTREAK
Callophrys sheridanii
Gossamer-wing family (Lycaenidae)
Quick ID: upper side grayish-brown; underwing emerald green (varies) with streak of white dots; lacks tails on hind wings
Wingspan: 0.86–1.14" Flight Season: March–June

The year 2009 was a landmark year for a small butterfly called Sheridan's green hairstreak, as this was the year that the state of Wyoming adopted it as the official state butterfly. This butterfly was named by the eminent entomologist William H. Edwards in 1877 to honor Gen. Philip H. Sheridan, who played a role in helping to establish the early military protection of Yellowstone National Park. Hairstreaks are small butterflies, and many sport threadlike tails on the hind wing, but these are lacking on Sheridan's green hairstreak. They are rapid fliers, flitting quickly about and perching on stems or flower tops with their wings closed. The caterpillars feed on buckwheat, *Eriogonum* sp., so watch for the adults depositing eggs on buckwheat plants.

WESTERN PINE ELFIN
Callophrys eryphon
Gossamer-wing family
(Lycaenidae)
Quick ID: reddish-brown; underwings
have jagged bands
Wingspan: 1–1.3"
Flight Season: May–June

One of the park's earliest spring butterflies, the western pine elfin emerges in spring when the willows are just starting to bloom. After mating, the female lays the eggs at the base of pine needles. When the caterpillars hatch, they feed on the young needles and catkins. They hibernate in chrysalid form and emerge the next spring. Look along LeHardy Rapids boardwalk for these and other early butterflies.

ROCKY MOUNTAIN DOTTED BLUE
Euphilotes ancilla
Gossamer-wing family
(Lycaenidae)
Quick ID: small; underwings light blue-gray
with squarish black spots and jagged orange
band; male—upper wing iridescent deep
blue with black border; female—upper
wing brown with light orange band; wings
edged with white
Wingspan: 0.6–1.0" Flight Season: May–August

Rocky Mountain dotted blue is a member of a complex of small blue butterflies called buckwheat blues, as their larvae feed on specific species of buckwheat; the adults stay close to their specific favorite buckwheat. Look for these butterflies nectaring on subalpine sulphur flower, *Eriogonum umbellatum*, that grows on Mount Washburn.

MORMON FRITILLARY
Speyeria mormonia
Brushfoot family (Nymphalidae)
Quick ID: medium-size fritillary; orange with black markings; rounded clubs on ends of antenna; forewings short and rounded; pale underneath with silvery spots
Wingspan: 1.5–2.4" Flight Season: June–September

In summer, the bright flower-filled meadows of Yellowstone attract a large number of butterflies called fritillaries. Fritillaries are sometimes mistaken for monarch butterflies as most are orange and black like monarchs, but once you start looking closely, you will notice that these butterflies do not have the same markings as monarchs. The word *fritillary* comes from the Latin word *fritillus*, which means "chessboard" or "dice box." Worldwide there are 14 species of greater fritillaries and 16 species of lesser fritillaries. You can see about 7 of these in Yellowstone, including the Mormon fritillary. The adults nectar on many flowers including rabbitbrush, *Chrysothamnus nauseosus*. Fritillaries can be seen throughout the park, including near Fishing Bridge, Sand Point, Bridge Bay, and Blacktail Plateau Drive.

GILLETTE'S CHECKERSPOT
Euphydryas gillettii
Brushfoot family (Nymphalidae)
Quick ID: medium-size; black with band of large orange spots and smaller white spots
Wingspan: 1.5–1.9" Flight Season: June–August

So eye-catching are the striking white, red, and yellow-orange patterns that checkerspots are often favorite butterflies to watch. Sometimes called Yellowstone checkerspot, Gillette's checkerspot has a limited distribution in Wyoming, Montana, Idaho, and British Columbia and Alberta, Canada. The preferred caterpillar food plant is bracted honeysuckle, *Lonicera involucrata*. In 1897 William Barnes described this butterfly but unfortunately did not record the person whom he honored with the species name *gillettii*. Lost for nearly a century, the identity of this mystery person may have been recently uncovered: The honor may belong to his benefactor, whose last name was Gillett and who happened to be his sister-in-law. The spelling of this butterfly may hence be changed back to its original Gillett's checkerspot, without the added *e*.

GREEN COMMA
Polygonia faunus
Brushfoot family (Nymphalidae)
Quick ID: upper wing reddish-brown with dark markings, dark borders with yellow spots; wing edges very jagged; underwing wavy gray and brown; green spots; C-shaped white marking on hind wing
Wingspan: 1.7–2.5" Flight Season: May–August

The wings of these butterflies look so jagged that they appear incapable of flight. However, it is this jagged, rough characteristic that aides in camouflage. The upper part of the wing is orangey red-brown, but when closed the undersides rival any hunter's camouflage clothing. Adults nectar on flowers and also ingest nutrients from carrion and dung.

MOURNING CLOAK
Nymphalis antiopa
Brushfoot family (Nymphalidae)
Quick ID: upper side purplish–dark brown bordered with a broad yellow band and blue spots; underside dark brown with dark striations
Wingspan: 3–4" Flight Season: May–October

One of the most widespread and easiest butterflies to identify is the mourning cloak. The brownish-purple wings are edged with a yellow border that fades to white. Mourning cloak caterpillars feed on willows, aspens, and cottonwood flowers. The adults will feed on flower nectar but prefer savory decaying matter and tree sap. These butterflies may live up to 1 year and can overwinter under tree bark or other protected places. It is for this reason that mourning cloaks are often one of the first butterflies to be seen in spring. In 2001 Montana designated this lovely butterfly as the official state insect.

HAYDEN'S RINGLET
Coenonympha haydenii
Brushfoot family (Nymphalidae)
Quick ID: on top, soft brown, no markings; soft grayish-brown underneath; hindwing has 5–7 black eyespots ringed with orange (the orange rings fade to yellow); low, skipping flight; male—darker gray-brown; female—lighter brown
Wingspan: 1.4–1.5"   Flight Season: late June–early August

Perhaps not the most impressive-looking butterfly, Hayden's ringlet is quite unique in the butterfly world. The entire world's range of this endemic butterfly is restricted to southwest Montana, southeast Idaho, and western Wyoming, including Yellowstone and Grand Teton National Parks. William Henry Edwards (1822–1909) was an entomologist who published the first major study of North American butterflies in 1847. In 1872, Edwards named this butterfly to honor Ferdinand Vandeveer Hayden, who in 1871 led a survey to study and explore the region that was to become Yellowstone National Park. These plain brown butterflies typically sit with folded wings so the orange-ringed eyespots are obvious. They fly slowly with a bouncy movement. Adults nectar on flowers and lay their eggs on grasses.

ONE-EYED SPHINX MOTH
Smerinthus cerisyi
Sphinx and hawkmoth family (Sphingidae)
Quick ID: large; heavy body; tan-brown with dark and light markings; forewing variably scalloped; hindwing mostly red with blue eyespot and central dark spot
Wingspan: 2.4–3.5" Flight Season: May–August

Sphinx moths such as this one have a unique defense mechanism. When startled they flash their wings open, revealing large eyespots hopefully realistic enough to frighten away the intruder. The adults don't feed at all, but the caterpillars feed on willows and cottonwoods in the park. In June, these large moths are often seen hanging on buildings, such as those at Lamar Buffalo Ranch.

POLICE CAR MOTH
Gnophaela vermiculata
Erebid moth family
(Erebidae)
Quick ID: all black with white patterns
on elongated wings
Wingspan: 2.1"
Flight Season: July–August

The striking black-and-white pattern on the wings of this moth generated their common name. They are sometimes called green lattice moths. While most moths are active at night, the police car moth is a day-flying tiger moth and can be easily viewed as they nectar on flowers near moist mountain meadows and open forests near water. The caterpillars feed on chiming bells or bluebells, *Mertensia* sp.

CLEARWING MOTH
Carmenta giliae
Clearwing moth family
(Sesiidae)
Quick ID: black with yellow bands;
wings appear clear with black veins
and orange spot; mothlike antennae;
fan-shaped tail
Wingspan: 1"
Flight Season: July–August

Not all things are as they seem, and the clearwing moth is one of these. This day-flying moth has evolved an amazing resemblance to wasps. Even though they are incapable of stinging, the possible threat wards off potential predators. Look for this mimic enjoying the flower nectar on Mount Washburn.

MAYFLY
Genus and species vary
Various families (Order: Ephemeroptera)
Quick ID: long, thin, soft bodies; veined wings held upright; long forewings overlap the hind wings; short antennae; large eyes; 2 threadlike cerci (tail-like appendages); nymphs (naiads)—dark; flattened head; 3 long cerci
Length: 0.04–1.18"

You may think that a mayfly's purpose in life is to land on you, but you are simply the thing that got in its way. With only a day or two to live out of water, the adults spend this precious time flying about quickly to find a mate. As adults, their mouthparts are nonfunctional, and they cannot eat or drink. Even though these insects can't eat, fish such as trout love to eat them. There are about 46 species of mayflies that have been documented in Yellowstone, with another 13 that have been found outside the park boundaries. Fly fishermen study the mayfly hatches and fashion their fishing flies to resemble these insects. This is an especially important skill to have in Yellowstone, where only artificial lures are allowed.

PADDLETAIL DARNER
Aeshna palmata
Darner family (Aeshnidae)
Quick ID: large; brown; male—blue markings; female—green markings
Length: 2.5–2.9"

The widespread and abundant paddletail darner is one of the most beautiful dragonflies on western shores. Hovering in midair on 4 translucent wings, they prey on a variety of insects including flies, mayflies, butterflies, moths, and mosquitos. The males have blue markings and the females have green markings. Look for these mini helicopters near marshes and lakes such as Trout Lake from July into early fall.

VIVID DANCER
Argia vivida
Narrow-winged damselfly family (Coenagrionidae)
Quick ID: male—bright blue
with black markings; female—
grayish-tan with black markings
Length: 1.2–1.6"

In 2009 the vivid dancer made history as the first damselfly to be named as an official state insect. Fourth-grade students throughout Nevada voted the beautiful blue damselfly to this prestigious honor. Damselflies are more slender than dragonflies, and they rest with their wings together above their bodies, whereas dragonflies hold their wings spread to the side. Damselflies eat many insects including mosquitoes, flies, and small moths. They will even glean aphids from plants.

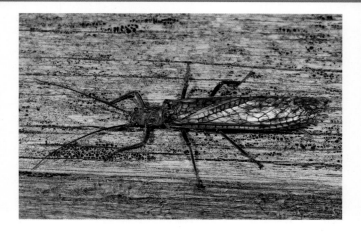

GIANT SALMONFLY
Pteronarcys californica
Giant stonefly family (Pteronarcyidae)
Quick ID: very large; body brownish on top, orange below; orange band behind head; long gray, tan, and clear netlike marked wings; front wings fold over shorter back wings; long antennae; 2 long tail parts; nymph—dark brown to black; 2 tails
Length: 1.2–2.0"

Although most people don't think of insects as thrilling, the incredible salmonfly hatch in Yellowstone is perhaps the most famous insect spectacle in the country. The hatch, which occurs from mid-June to early July, is an exciting time for both trout and trout anglers. Salmonflies are large, dark stoneflies with a bright orange abdomen. They begin life as eggs that hatch into nymphs, and they remain in cool, fast-moving waters for about 3 years. When the adults crawl out of the water, they shed their exoskeleton on rocks or trees and emerge as winged adults. Their only task is to mate and lay their eggs on the water. The timing of the hatch is dependent on temperature and generally occurs in an upstream pattern.

TWO-STRIPED GRASSHOPPER
Melanoplus bivittatus bivittatus
Short-horned grasshopper family (Acrididae)
Quick ID: large; light brownish-yellow; 2 yellow stripes along sides of top; dark stripe on rear leg
Length: 1.2–2.2"

Grasshoppers are a very diverse group of insects; almost 700 species can be found in the western states. Although most grasshoppers are never noticed, the two-striped grasshopper is a relatively large grasshopper and attracts attention from June to October. They eat mostly weeds and broad-leaved plants, but their love of grasses and crops can sometimes cause damage on farms and in gardens.

150

WATER STRIDER
Aquarius sp.
Water strider family (Gerridae)
Quick ID: long, thin body; brownish; 3 jointed sets of legs (6) with the front legs much shorter than the others; 2 short antenna
Length: 0.1–0.6"

This is one of the favorite insects of science teachers everywhere, as the principle of water tension is demonstrated vividly by the ability of this insect to walk on water. They have fine water-repellant hairs on their feet that keep them from sinking through the surface. Although water striders look like a cross between a large mosquito and a spider, they are not spiders at all but true insects. They use their short front legs to grab prey such as mosquito larvae and other insects. Water striders are harmless to people.

TUMBLEBUG

Canthon sp.
Scarab beetle family
(Scarabaeidae)
Quick ID: black; smooth; chunky-looking
beetle with prominent head shield
Length: 0.2–0.8"

Although it sounds gross, we should all be glad that tumble-bugs, or dung beetles, feed on dung, else we would soon have a major problem. Tumblebugs roll dung into round balls and either store it for food or lay their eggs in the dung ball. Dung beetles navigate at night using the Milky Way to orient themselves.

ORNATE CHECKERED BEETLE

Trichodes ornatus
Checkered beetle family
(Cleridae)
Quick ID: long black body; yellow
bands on wing covering; covered all
over with short, bristly hairs
Length: 0.2–0.6"

The ornate checkered beetle derives its name from its colorful black and yellow markings. They can be seen eating pollen on flowers in areas such as Sheepeater Cliff. The bristly hairs covering the beetles aid the transfer of pollen from flower to flower. They are also known to prey on other insects.

GRAND HYDROPSYCHID CADDISFLY

Arctopsyche grandis
Netspinning caddisfly family
(Hydropsychidae)
Quick ID: dull brownish to yellowish, mothlike,
2 pairs of wings with small hairs, wings held
tentlike, long antennae
Length: body about 1"

There are many species of caddisflies in Yellowstone, and anglers study the minute details as they prepare their flies to grab the attention of trout. Caddisflies have 4 metamorphic life stages: egg, larva, pupa, and adult. The aquatic wormlike larvae can be free swimming, or some build a protective case made of stones, twigs, or leaves (inset).

153

EPHYDRID FLY
Ephydra bruesi
Brine fly family
(Ephydridae)
Quick ID: small; blackish
Length: 0.09–0.35"

One of the most unique food webs in the world involves a small fly called an ephydrid fly that flourishes in the warm water running from hot springs in the park. The ephydrid flies feed on the abundant cyanobacteria that form the colorful mats surrounding the geysers and hot springs. Other insects such as spiders, dragonflies, and tiger beetles then feed upon the flies. Further up the food chain, mountain bluebirds enjoy the insects, as do shorebirds called killdeer, which run about on long legs, snatching up not only the ephydrid flies but also the insects that are there to feed on the flies.

HUNT'S BUMBLEBEE
Bombus huntii
Bee family (Apidae)
Quick ID: medium size; black; yellow hairs on face and body; bright orange toward end of body
Length: 0.42–0.54"

Bumblebees and other bees play an important role in the pollination of plants. Bees are susceptible to diseases that can devastate the colony. There are several bumblebee species in the park, including a few that are high-altitude specialists surviving in the harsh environment where most insects can't live.

154

HOBO SPIDER
Eratigena agrestis
Funnel weaver family (Agelenidae)
Quick ID: medium size; light-brown elongated body; dark-brown patterns; 2 distinct zig-zag herringbone patterns on top; legs evenly colored with black bristles (no rings around legs); males have enlarged palps (appendages)
Length: body 0.3–0.6"; about 1–2" leg span

Recently introduced into the Pacific Northwest, hobo spiders have a bad reputation for being aggressive and dangerous, both of which are invalidated beliefs. These spiders only bite when they feel threatened or unintentionally contacted. Hobo spiders construct funnel-shaped webs in holes or cracks or in shrubs.

Comparison of Spiders and Insects

	Spider	Insect
Eyes	8 simple eyes	2 compound eyes
Antenna	No antennae—uses bristles or hairs on legs to sense things	2 antennae—uses antennae to sense things
Wings	No wings	4, 2, or none
Legs	4 pairs (8 legs)	3 pairs (6 legs)
Body parts	2	3
Abdomen	Unsegmented	Segmented

NEW ZEALAND MUD SNAIL
Potamopyrgus antipodarum
Mud snail family
(Hydrobiidae)
Quick ID: small; brownish; spiral-shaped shell that coils to the right; 5 or 6 coils
Length: 0.16–0.24"

A world away, the New Zealand mud snail is native to New Zealand. They were introduced into Montana in the late 1980s and quickly moved into Yellowstone. They are primarily spread by humans when the mud snails stick to fishing gear. These nonnative invasive snails reproduce quickly and outcompete native snails and invertebrates that are the natural food for many native fish, including trout. They have no natural predators. Take caution not to transport these snails into other waters.

MICROBES
Various
Various domains
Quick ID: colors vary
Length: microscopic

Microscopic organisms create some of the most interesting colors and patterns seen in Yellowstone (see photos opposite). Large microbial mats form around hot springs in colorful patterns of green, orange, yellow, pink, and various shades of brown, white, and black. Some produce overpowering rotten-egg smells, and some look thick and slimy. Bacteria, viruses, cyanobacteria, and algae can be found in various pools. Some organisms are part of the ancient Archaea domain and are thought to be among the earliest forms of life on Earth. Some of these organisms are called thermophiles and grow in high temperatures and acidic conditions.

Comparison of Conifers in Yellowstone

	Lodgepole Pine	Limber Pine	Whitebark Pine	Engelmann Spruce	Rocky Mountain Alpine Fir	Rocky Mountain Douglas-Fir	Rocky Mountain Juniper
Growth form	20–80'; dense stands	30–50'; ridge tops and rocky foothills	20–50'; high elevations only; short crooked trunk; irregular spreading crown	80–100'; drooping spreading branches form spire	50–80'; slender, spire-like; branches near ground	80–120'; long, slightly drooping branches; pyramid shape	16–50'; bushy, often with multiple stems, low elevations
Needles (leaves)	1–3" bundles of 2, often twisted	1.5–2.5" dense bundles of 5 near ends of branches	1.5–2.75" bundles of 5 crowded at ends of twigs	1" single, stiff, sharp, square-sided needles roll between fingers	1" needles tend to grow upward; flat needles will not roll easily between fingers	1" bluish-green, flat, flexible, soft, blunt; flat needles will not roll between fingers	0.06", flat, scale-like (sharply pointed when young)
Cones	2", appear lop-sided, sharp spines	5", egg-shaped, thick scales, green when young	1.5–3.25", egg-shaped, thick scales with sharp edge (purple when young)	1.5–2.5", downward hanging at end of twig; scales narrow and angular with irregular edge	2.25–4", upright, purplish often waxy resin-coated	2–3.5", narrow scales with 3-pointed, protruding bracts	0.25", blue-black berrylike cones with waxy coating on female plant; cones on males inconspicuous
Bark	flaky, thick, gray (orange-brown on young trees)	dark brown, plates (light gray, smooth on young trees)	whitish-gray, thin, scaly	grayish- to red-brown, thin, scaly	silvery, smooth, resin blisters, furrows show underlying red-brown layer	reddish-brown, thick, furrowed bark	reddish-brown, scaly

ROCKY MOUNTAIN ALPINE FIR
Abies bifolia
Pine family (Pinaceae)
Quick ID: evergreen; upward-curving, soft, flat, 1" long, white-lined needles; 2.25–4"
erect purple cones covered with waxy pitch; silvery, thin, smooth bark with resin blisters,
furrows show red-brown layer underneath
Height: 50–80'

At high altitudes in the park, such as Mount Washburn and Craig Pass,
the tall spire-like tips of Rocky Mountain alpine fir point dramatically
upward into the clear Wyoming skies. The scales of the upright cones
drop to the ground when mature or as leftovers from seed meals of squirrels and chipmunks. These scales were gathered by American Indians,
pounded into fat, and served as a delicacy. Conifer needles, including
firs, were made into a poultice and applied to the chest to cure coughs
and colds. The gummy pitch secretions were used on wounds as an
antiseptic. Through chemical analysis and other characteristics, Rocky
Mountain alpine fir is the species of fir found in Yellowstone rather than
subalpine fir, *A. lasiocarpa*, which is found in Washington and Oregon.

ENGELMANN SPRUCE
Picea engelmannii
Pine family (Pinaceae)
Quick ID: evergreen; dark green, 4-sided, 1" long, sharp needles with whitish lines; cylindrical 1.5–2.5" cones with irregular edge thin grayish or purplish-brown; grayish redbrown bark scales loosely attached
Height: 80–100'

Tall spire-like Engelmann spruce are common in the spruce and fir forests of the park. The needles are shorter and stiffer than those of fir, and when touched they are sharp on the tips. You can use the alliteration of the description to help you remember this tree, as they have "sharp square spruce" needles. The name of this tree honors George Engelmann (1809–1884), a German physician and botanist who worked with Harvard botanist Asa Gray to document the plants of the western states. High in vitamin C, spruce needles were made into a tea to prevent and treat scurvy, which was a problem in winter and on long ship voyages. It was also mixed with molasses and yeast to make beer.

WHITEBARK PINE
Pinus albicaulis
Pine family (Pinaceae)
Quick ID: evergreen; high elevations only; short, crooked trunk with irregular spreading crown, dull green needles 1.5–2.75" with faint white lines in bundles of 5 crowded at the end of twigs; 1.5–3.25" cones, rounded thick scales with sharp edge; thin whitish-gray, scaly bark
Height: 20–50'

The harsh high-altitude environment takes its toll on this evergreen that often becomes gnarly and stunted from exposure to the unforgiving elements. The large, nutritious seeds of whitebark pine are valued as an important food source for many types of wildlife, including grizzly bears and Clark's nutcrackers, which are one of the few birds that can open the tough cones, and these crafty birds cache the seeds for winter. The unretrieved seeds play an important role in the establishment of new whitebark pines. The pine nuts were also an important food for American Indians, who roasted and mixed them with dried berries to preserve for winter food. To find this high-elevation tree, look at Dunraven Pass and Craig Pass in the park.

LODGEPOLE PINE
Pinus contorta
Pine family (Pinaceae)
Quick ID: evergreen; bundles of 2 often twisted needles, 1–3", sharply pointed; 2" long cones with raised, rounded scales, many remain closed for years; thin, scaly bark
Height: 20–80'

Of the 7 species of conifers in Yellowstone, the lodgepole pine is the most prevalent, with about 80 percent of the forested areas made up of this species. In some areas of the park, the black remnants of past forest fires are gradually being replaced by new growth of young lodgepoles. The cones often remain on the trees for many years until high heat from a fire causes them to open and drop their tightly held seeds to the ground, where they can sprout to regenerate the forest. This type of heat-exposed seed release occurs in a "serotinous" cone. American Indians used the long, straight wood for building lodges and tepees. Lodgepole pine is the official tree of Alberta, Canada.

LIMBER PINE
Pinus flexilis
Pine family (Pinaceae)
Quick ID: evergreen; 1.5–2.5" long 3-sided needles in bundles of 5 with white lines on all surfaces; egg-shaped 5" long cones with rounded scales that have a blunt tip; gray-brown, scaly bark
Height: 30–50'

Along with Rocky Mountain juniper, limber pines are found in dry places at lower elevations in the park, such as the Mammoth area. Although slow growing, this tree can withstand dry, windy conditions and therefore may grow for hundreds of years. Just as it does with whitebark pine, Clark's nutcracker, *Nucifraga columbiana*, gathers the nutrient-rich pine nuts to store for the winter. This mutualistic relationship between birds and the limber pine is vital as the seeds of limber pine rely on birds such as the nutcracker and pinyon jays, *Gymnorhinus cyanocephalus*, unlike most pines that disperse their seeds in the wind. The pine nuts from the cones of limber pine were also an important source of food for American Indians.

163

ROCKY MOUNTAIN DOUGLAS-FIR
Pseudotsuga menziesii
Pine family (Pinaceae)
Quick ID: evergreen; green, flat, soft, fragrant, needles 1" spreading in 2 rows that resemble a bottlebrush; 2–3.5" long cones and narrow scales with 3-pointed protruding bracts; reddish-brown, thick, furrowed bark
Height: 80–120'

With this tree, the name says a lot. Douglas-fir was named to honor the Scottish botanist David Douglas, but the name is hyphenated as it resembles a fir but is not a true fir. The genus name, *Pseudotsuga* means "false hemlock." The species name, *menziesii*, honors yet another botanist, Archibald Menzies, who first documented the tree on Vancouver Island in 1791. Douglas-fir is easy to identify by the unique 3-pointed bracts that stick out of the cones. An American Indian story associates the bracts with the tail and hind feet of a mouse that ran into the cone to hide from a fox. Outside the park, Douglas-fir is valued for lumber because of its strength and straight grain.

ROCKY MOUNTAIN JUNIPER
Juniperus scopulorum
Cedar family (Cupressaceae)
Quick ID: evergreen; small tree or erect shrub often with multiple stems; small scalelike needles; berrylike green or dark blue cones; reddish-brown to gray scaly bark
Height: 16–50'

Rocky Mountain juniper is a small tree that grows in rocky cliffs or along hillsides at lower elevations of the park. It is a common tree in the Mammoth area at the North Entrance of the park. The flat, scalelike leaves provide great cover for small birds, including warblers and Townsend's solitaire, *Myadestes townsendi*, which tends to claim one tree as its own. Townsend's solitaire loves to eat the ripe pea-size, fleshy, blue berrylike cones and will fiercely guard its claim. Only the female plant produces these berrylike cones; the male plant produces inconspicuous, pollen-bearing cones at the tips of branches. American Indians burned the twigs as incense. Parts of the plant were also used to treat arthritis, colds, dandruff, and venereal disease.

NARROWLEAF COTTONWOOD
Populus angustifolia
Willow family (Salicaceae)
Quick ID: deciduous; lance-shaped 2–5" leaves that are finely serrated, yellowish-green flowers in 1.5–4" long spikes called catkins that appear before leaves; bark is gray and furrowed
Height: 45–60'

Visitors entering the park from Gardiner, Montana, at the North Entrance may notice narrowleaf cottonwood trees that grow along the North Entrance road and Mammoth area. The leaves are long, narrow, and very willowlike. The sticky balsam-scented buds help separate this tree from willows; the buds were used as chewing gum by American Indians. In spring, when the spikes of flowers are finished blooming, they are replaced by clouds of tiny seeds that float through the air like cottony puffballs. During the winter, American Indians used the wood of narrowleaf cottonwood for fire and to build shelters. The inner bark was mixed with other plants and smoked in a mixture called kinnikinnick. In Lamar Valley, groves of narrowleaf cottonwood provide shelter for grazing bison and nesting raptors.

QUAKING ASPEN
Populus tremuloides
Willow family (Salicaceae)
Quick ID: deciduous; broad, heart-shaped to round leaves, 1–3" with finely toothed margins; flowers in 1–3" drooping spikes called catkins; smooth, whitish-gray bark often with dark scars
Height: 40–75'

Even though most of the trees in Yellowstone are dark pines, firs, and spruces that create the vast conifer forests, scattered throughout the park are lovely groves of quaking aspen. Sometimes called trembling aspen, the leaves are attached with flexible stems that quiver like a multitude of tiny kites with the slightest breeze. Aspen roots spread laterally underground, producing vertical shoots called suckers. Genetically identical to the parent tree, the young shoots grow into clones, with many members sharing the same root system. Because quaking aspen are all one organism, the leaves turn color in fall at one time, creating patches of brilliant yellows and oranges that provide stunning scenes for inspiring photographs, especially when backlit by the setting sun.

BLACK CHOKECHERRY
Prunus virginiana var. *melanocarpa*
Rose family (Rosaceae)
Quick ID: deciduous; small tree or shrub sometimes forming thickets; alternate 2–4"
leaves that are oval with fine serrations, dark green above and pale below; white flowers
in loose 3–5" cylindrical clusters; small red to purple fruits; smooth, gray-brown bark
Height: 12–25'

Sometimes called common or western chokecherry, black chokecherry is a small tree or large shrub that blooms in late May or early June. The fra-

grant white flowers are followed by red fruits that mature to purple in late summer. Parts of the plant are poisonous, especially the new growth, causing choking and difficulty breathing. When ripe, the fruits are made into jams and syrup. American Indians ground the berries and mixed them with meat and other food to make pemmican, which was dried and used as a portable high-energy food. Black chokecherry is one of the deciduous trees in the Mammoth campground; you might see the silken tents of western tent caterpillars that feed on the leaves.

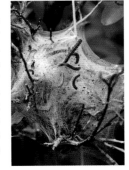

COMMON JUNIPER
Juniperus communis var. *depressa*
Cypress family (Cupressaceae)
Quick ID: evergreen; low, spreading branches; sharply pointed leaves, 0.25–0.75" in whorls around stem; round bluish-black berrylike cones with whitish chalky dusting; bark reddish-brown in shreds
Height: 1–4'

Common juniper, or ground juniper, is a low spreading evergreen, while the taller Rocky Mountain juniper, *J. scopulorum*, reaches tree size. Junipers have fruits that look like berries but are technically cones with fleshy, fused scales. The blue-black cones, or "juniper berries," are consumed by birds who widely distribute the seeds in their droppings. The astringent juniper cones are used to flavor gin; the word *gin* is derived from the French word for juniper. The crushed dried berries were used to flavor meats and other foods. Various parts of the plant have been used to treat coughs, tuberculosis, and asthma. The crushed berries were also used as a contraceptive.

BIG SAGEBRUSH
Artemisia tridentata
Aster family (Asteraceae)
Quick ID: rounded shrub with branched woody trunks; greenish-silver hairy leaves with 3 blunt teeth, creamy yellow flowers on narrow stalks
Height: 1–8'

Big sagebrush is such an important and widespread western plant that in 1917 Nevada designated it as the official state flower. Sagebrush is very nutritious and is a valuable plant for many species of wildlife, including deer, moose, elk, and bighorn sheep. In Yellowstone, pronghorns enjoy nibbling on big sagebrush, while mule deer prefer fringed sage, *A. frigida*. Highly aromatic and filled with volatile oils, sagebrush is quite flammable and has been used by humans to light firewood. American Indians used sagebrush in a multitude of ways, including as an antiseptic wash for wounds, a gargle for sore throats, and a remedy for headaches. They made a poultice from the leaves for soothing aches and pains, and it was used as a remedy for diarrhea.

RABBITBRUSH
Ericameria sp.
Aster family (Asteraceae)
Quick ID: mounding shrub with slender, erect, flexible branches with matted hairs; small flower heads in dense, narrow clusters; narrow leaves
Height: 2–3'

Rabbitbrush is a variable shrub found in the western states in dry sagebrush areas. It is conspicuous when it blooms in late summer, showing off bright yellow heads of wispy flowers. Both yellow rabbitbrush, *Chrysothamnus viscidiflorus*, and rubber rabbitbrush, *E. nauseosa*, are found in the park, with subspecies of each. Also found in the park are similar plants with yellow flowers, whitestem goldenbush, *E. discoidea*, and singlehead goldenbush, *E. suffruticosa*. American Indians used rabbitbrush for making a yellow dye and as a chewing gum. Rubber rabbitbrush contains a resin that is  under study for potential biomaterial and bioenergy uses. It is also being researched as an alternate source of rubber for people with latex allergies.

171

BLACK ELDERBERRY
Sambucus racemosa var. *melanocarpa*
Moschatel family (Adoxaceae)
Quick ID: compound opposite pinnate leaves; creamy white flowers in clusters; purplish-black berrylike fruits (drupes); reddish-brown, warty bark
Height: 3–6'

Black elderberry or Rocky Mountain elder is a variety of red elderberry, *S. racemosa*. In the park, it is found along the edges of moist meadows or along streams. Although all parts of the plant contain cyanide and are toxic, the ripe cooked berries of many species are used to make jelly, pies, tea, and wine. American Indians used an infusion of the bark and roots to induce vomiting and as a laxative. Studies are under way to research the antiviral properties of elderberries, as their use has been shown to reduce the effects and duration of influenza. The similar-looking Cascade mountain ash, *Sorbus scopulina* var. *scopulina*, also has white flowers in clusters, but it has alternate leaves rather than the opposite leaves of elderberries.

UTAH HONEYSUCKLE
Lonicera utahensis
Honeysuckle family (Caprifoliaceae)
Quick ID: slender, spreading branches; opposite egg-shaped leaves; pale-yellow nodding tubular flowers in pairs; rounded bright red berries in pairs joined at the base
Height: 3–6'

Blooming in June, the pale yellow flowers hang downward near the tip of the stems of Utah honeysuckle. Sometimes called red twinberry, the enticing bright red berries often draw attention but may be toxic to humans. Bearberry honeysuckle, *L. caerulea*, which is also found in the park, has small yellow flowers that are covered by reddish-brown bracts at the base and the fruit is black. Birds, chipmunks, and other animals eat the berries of both species. The genus, *Lonicera*, is named to honor Adam Lonicer (1528–1586), a German physician and botanist who studied and wrote numerous papers and books about herbs and other plants.

UTAH SNOWBERRY
Symphoricarpos oreophilus var. *utahensis*
Honeysuckle family (Caprifoliaceae)
Quick ID: opposite, round to oblong 1–2" leaves; light pink, tubular flowers; fruits are white berries
Height: 1–4'

The round white berries easily identify snowberry. Although birds and animals eat the white popcorn-like berries, do not try them as they can cause severe vomiting and dizziness in humans. Sometimes called ghost berry, it was believed that the white berries possessed spiritual powers, and they were hung near cradles to protect children from evil spirits. American Indians crushed the leaves to make a poultice for sores, and the bark was mixed with wild rose to make an eyewash. The fruits were used for injured eyes, and an infusion of the twigs was used to treat fevers. Two similar species of snowberry are found in Yellowstone: western snowberry, *S. occidentalis*, and common snowberry, *S. albus* var. *laevigatus*.

BLACK GREASEWOOD
Sarcobatus vermiculatus
Greasewood family (Sarcobataceae)
Quick ID: branching; branches taper to spiny point; thick, narrow green to yellowish-green, rubbery, 0.5–2" leaves; inconspicuous greenish flowers; ½' fruits are flat with papery wings
Height: 2–8'

Not many plants can survive in the dry desertlike conditions such as those found at the North Entrance near Gardiner, Montana, but with an incredibly long taproot, sometimes reaching over 20 feet in the soil, black greasewood endures. Relatively high in protein and sodium, black grease-

wood is used as a food source by pronghorn and jackrabbits. Its low-hanging branches also provide cover for these mammals and birds. High in potassium oxalates, this plant can cause death if animals eat too much all at once. Black greasewood was formerly included in the goosefoot family, Chenopodiaceae; the strong wood was used for digging and as firewood. Several plants are commonly called greasewood, some of which are made into medicinal poultices using the greasy sap.

WILLOW SP.
Salix sp.
Willow family (Salicaceae)
Quick ID: shrub with numerous stems; long oblong or egg-shaped leaves pointed at tip; bark often shiny
Height: 0.5–18'

Over 25 species of willows can be found in the Yellowstone area, and identification of the various species is often a challenge for even the most experienced botanist. To separate willow species you need to look at growth details such as leaf hairs or glands, width and length of leaves, toothed or untoothed leaf margins, and presence of leaf stems called stipules. Willows form dense thickets along streams and wetlands in the park, creating important shelter habitats for numerous animals, including moose, elk, and many birds. Willow leaves contain a compound that was used as the first headache treatment. A few of the species found in the park include dusky willow, *S. melanopsis*; Geyer's willow, *S. geyeriana*; and greenleaf willow, *S. lasiandra*.

BEARBERRY
Arctostaphylos uva-ursi
Heath family (Ericaceae)
Quick ID: spreading undercover shrub; spoon-shaped leaves; pink bell-shaped flowers; bright red fruit
Height: 6–12"

Bearberry is a short, spreading shrub sometimes carpeting the forest floor. Its common name, kinnikinnick, comes from an Algonquian word meaning "that which is mixed." After drying the leaves and mixing them with other plants, American Indians used the mixture as a tobacco to smoke. The leaves were also used medicinally to treat a variety of ailments, especially urinary disorders. It was used as an astringent and a relieving soak for those suffering from hemorrhoids.

The bright red berries (drupes) are mealy but were often dried and used in food mixtures. The fruits spoil slowly and often remain on the branches into spring, when they are eaten by birds, bears, and other mammals.

GROUSE WHORTLEBERRY
Vaccinium scoparium
Heath family (Ericaceae)
Quick ID: small understory shrub; pale green, 0.6" long leaves; pink, urn-shaped flowers; red berries
Height: 3–8"

Resembling small whisk brooms, grouse whortleberry often blankets the forest floor under conifers. Several species of similar berry-producing plants are found in the park, including dwarf bilberry, *V. cespitosum*; huckleberry, *V. membranaceum*; blueberry, *V. scoparium*; and whortleberry, *V. myrtillus* var. *oreophilum*. The berries were collected by American Indians and early settlers for use as a delicious food source. The berries were made into desserts, jams, jellies, and wine. *Vaccinium* is the Latin name for "blueberry"; *whortle* is derived from the Anglo-Saxon word *wyrtil*, which means "a small shrub." Also called bilberry, the word *huckleberry* derives from the Middle English slang for "person of little consequence," apparently referring to the small size of the berries.

THINLEAF ALDER
Alnus incana ssp. *tenuifolia*
Birch family (Betulaceae)
Quick ID: alternate 2–4" egg-shaped leaves with double-toothed margins; flowers on hanging catkins, female catkins persist as woody 0.5–1" cone-like structures; smooth, gray bark
Height: 20–33'

Thinleaf or mountain alder is a tall, deciduous shrub or small tree that is found along rivers and streams in the park. Thinleaf alder is a subspecies of gray alder. The roots of alders have swollen nodules that contain symbiotic nitrogen-fixing bacteria that convert essential nitrogen into a form that can be used by the plant. Alders and birches both have separate male and female flower clusters that hang in catkins. The female catkins stay on the tree and persist as woody cone-like structures. American Indians used thinleaf alder for a wide variety of uses: The wood was used to make bows, and the bark was used to make an orangey-brown dye.

CREEPING BARBERRY
Mahonia repens
Barberry family (Berberidaceae)
Quick ID: evergreen; leathery holly-like leaves; small yellow flowers; dark blue berries
Height: 1–3'

Today we rely on drugstores and pharmacies for our health-care needs, but before modern times people often depended on plants for healing purposes. This ethnobotanical knowledge was passed down through the generations, and certain plants were well known for their medicinal value. Creeping barberry, or creeping Oregon grape, is one of the plants that was used in many ways by American Indians. The roots were used for various medicinal purposes, including as a cough medicine, an anti-septic for wounds and boils, and for stomach ailments. When pro-cessed, the bark produced a yellow dye that was used to color baskets and clothing. The tart blue berries are still gathered today to make treats such as desserts, jams, jellies, and refreshing teas and cold drinks.

GOLDEN CURRANT
Ribes aureum var. *aureum*
Gooseberry family (Grossulariaceae)
Quick ID: glossy, shallowly lobed fan-shaped leaves turn red in fall; fragrant yellow flowers; dark yellow to blackish berries
Height: 6–9'

Of the 8 species of currants that can be found in the park, golden currant is one of the loveliest. In spring, the golden-yellow flowers fill the air with a clove-like fragrance. Unfortunately, gooseberries and currants often harbor an introduced fungus, *Cronartium ribicola*, which causes white pine blister rust. It cannot be passed from pine to pine but requires a secondary host, including members of the *Ribes* genus of gooseberries and currants. This rust is of great concern to park biologists, who are studying its effect on the high-altitude whitebark pine, *Pinus albicaulis*. Recently, scientists discovered that the rust is also harbored by two common wildflowers, sickletop lousewort, *Pedicularis racemosa*, and scarlet paintbrush, *Castilleja miniata*.

181

WHISKY CURRANT

Ribes cereum var. *pedicellare*

Gooseberry family (Grossulariaceae)

Quick ID: many twisted branches; glossy, shallowly lobed fan-shaped leaves; pink tubular flowers; red, sticky fruit; gray stems lack spines and prickles

Height: 1–6'

Currants or gooseberries are small rounded shrubs with rounded, lobed leaves. Delightful pink tubular flowers are followed by fleshy, round fruits, often with prickles. The genus *Ribes* includes gooseberries and currants, and some species have spines and prickles, while others lack them. Sometimes the shrubs with spines are called gooseberries, and the spineless ones are called currants. Currants are used for making jams and desserts. One variety of currant found in the park, *R. cereum* var. *pedicellare*, is called whisky currant or simply wax currant. It used to be referred to as *R. inebrians*, as the fermented fruits of some currants are used to make wine and alcoholic beverages. The species name, *cereum*, means "waxy" and refers to the glossy leaves.

RED OSIER DOGWOOD
Cornus sericea
Dogwood family (Cornaceae)
Quick ID: opposite leaves 2–4", egg-shaped, pointed veins curve to merge on margin, red in fall; 4 small, whitish petals on flowers in flat clusters; whitish berries; reddish to light-brown bark
Height: 3–10'

Red osier or redosier dogwood is a loosely spreading, multistemmed shrub that often forms dense thickets. Unlike the showy bracts of many dogwoods, the whitish flowers are dainty and small. It is most noticeable in fall when the leaves turn brilliant burnt red in a colorful farewell to summer. Red osier dogwood is an important source of food for many animals, including birds, chipmunks, elk, and moose. The inner bark was used by American Indians in a tobacco mixture. The stems were used for basket weaving and to make fishing nets and arrows. The word *osier* comes from the French word for a long, new shoot, and *dogwood* is derived from the Scandinavian word *dag*, which means "skewer."

183

RUSSET BUFFALOBERRY
Shepherdia canadensis
Oleaster family (Elaeagnaceae)

Quick ID: loosely branched shrub; opposite, elliptical, thick, leathery, greenish-gray leaves with scurfy brown dots underneath; tiny yellow flowers have 4 parts; red berries; branches lack spines

Height: 3–6'

Russet buffaloberry is an unassuming shrub that is associated with a dessert that you would not normally find in the wilderness: ice cream. American Indians gathered the bitter, ripe berries, whipped them into a froth, and added sweet fruits to serve as a unique ice-cream dessert. You didn't want to eat too much as the saponins that create the foam could cause stomachaches. Various parts of the plant were used medicinally for indigestion, eyewashes, and heart attacks, and to induce childbirth. The inner bark was used to make a plaster bandage for broken bones. The berries were so valuable that sometimes they were smoked, dried, and used for trading purposes. Black and grizzly bears eat the ripe berries, which are high in protein.

SNOWBRUSH CEANOTHUS
Ceanothus velutinus
Buckthorn family (Rhamnaceae)
Quick ID: small, white, fragrant flowers in dense clusters; alternate, oval, 1.5–3.5" ever-green leaves with fine serrations, often curling, shiny and sticky above, fuzzy below; brown seedpods with 3 parts
Height: 2–6'

Thickets of snowbrush ceanothus often form stunning floral displays of creamy white flowers in spring. Snowbrush plants can reproduce quickly after a fire, as the seeds can remain dormant in the soil for over 100 years. Ceanothus shrubs are one of the few plants besides legumes that contain nitrogen-fixing bacteria in their root nodules, which change nitrogen into a usable form for the plant. The aromatic leaves were used as deodorant and a soap. The leaves contain saponins that, when mixed with water, create suds, providing a gentle body wash.

SASKATOON SERVICEBERRY
Amelanchier alnifolia
Rose family (Rosaceae)
Quick ID: spreading shrub; alternate, oval 1–2" leaves;
white, star-shaped flowers; dark purple fruit
Height: 3–10'

One of the first shrubs to bloom in spring, the white star-shaped blossoms of Saskatoon serviceberry burst forth like popcorn covering the branches. Also known as western serviceberry or shadbush, the tender stems and leaves are heavily browsed by elk, deer, moose, and bighorn sheep. Birds enjoy the berries, as do humans. American Indians cooked the nutritious berries (drupes) in a variety of foods, including stews, meat dishes, and pemmican. The berries were used medicinally as eye- and ear drops and were also used to make a purple dye. The strong branches were shaped into arrows, spears, and pipe stems.

SHRUBBY CINQUEFOIL
Dasiphora fruticosa
Rose family (Rosaceae)
Quick ID: many-branched shrub; yellow buttercup-like flowers with 5 petals; numerous leaves with 3–9 divided leaflets with long white hairs; hairy fruits; fibrous bark
Height: 1–4'

A common shrub found in Yellowstone, shrubby cinquefoil has bright yellow buttercup-like flowers that bloom from June through late August or early September. Cinquefoil comes from a French word that means "5 leaves" and refers to the 5 parts of the flower. The taxonomy of this plant has been undergoing systematic changes, and synonyms include *Potentilla fruticosa*, *Dasiphora floribunda*, and *Pentaphylloides floribunda*. American Indians used the leaves as a spice, and the dry, flaky bark was used as tinder for starting fires. Shrubby cinquefoil is common in moist meadows and subalpine regions of the park such as Mount Washburn.

ANTELOPE BITTERBRUSH
Purshia tridentata
Rose family (Rosaceae)
Quick ID: wedge-shaped leaves with 3-lobed tips; 5-petaled pale-yellow flowers with deep-yellow stamens in center; slender, leathery fruit
Height: 4–8'

In May and June the sweetly scented aroma from the creamy yellow blossoms of antelope bitterbrush sweetens the air. First collected by Meriwether Lewis on the Lewis and Clark Expedition in 1806, antelope bitterbrush was named to honor a German botanist named Frederick Pursh (1774–1820), who was instrumental in studying the collection of plants that had been collected by Lewis and Clark. Even though the foliage is bitter, this shrub is one of the most important browse plants for animals. It was also used by American Indians as a tonic, for skin problems, and for venereal diseases. The seedpods were also used to make a purple stain for wood.

THIMBLEBERRY
Rubus parviflorus
Rose family (Rosaceae)
Quick ID: large leaves, up to 8", with 5 sharply toothed lobes; gray-brown peeling bark; stems with hairy glands but no prickles; white flowers with 5 petals and yellow-tipped stamens that form a ring in the center; wide, red thimble-shaped fruit
Height: 3–6'

Thimbleberry is a noticeable shrub with large leaves, papery white flowers, and red raspberrylike berries. A member of the rose family, the thimbleberry has white flowers that resemble those of a wild rose. The leaves of thimbleberry look like large, soft maple leaves and American Indians often used them in cooking to line fire pits or as a mat on which to dry berries. The tasty red fruits were eaten fresh or used to make jams and jellies; they were also dried for use in winter. Some American Indians harvested the young shoots in spring and cooked them like asparagus. The plant was used medicinally to treat vomiting and diarrhea. Perhaps one of the first acne medications, the leaves and roots were used to treat pimples.

WOODS' ROSE
Rosa woodsii
Rose family (Rosaceae)
Quick ID: pink flowers with 5 petals; leaves
are compound with 5–9 leaflets; the
fruit (hip) resembles a berry but has many small seeds
Height: 3–6'

The fleshy red fruits of roses are called "hips" and are commonly used
for making jellies, jams, and tea. Rose hips are well known for their high
vitamin C content, but they are also a good source of calcium, manganese,
and vitamins A, E, and K. American Indians used the roots to make a
medicine for colds and diarrhea. Various parts of the plant were also used
to heal sores, wounds, and burns. Birds and mammals eat the hips and
spread the seeds in their droppings far from the parent plant. The shrub
is named for a British botanist, Joseph Woods (1776–1864), who was an
expert in roses. A beautiful related rose, *R. acicularis*, was adopted as the
official flower of Alberta, Canada.

SHINYLEAF SPIREA
Spiraea betulifolia var. *lucida*
Rose family (Rosaceae)
Quick ID: tiny white flowers in clusters 2–5" across with extended fuzzy stamens; alternate oval 1–3" shiny, coarsely toothed leaves; reddish bark; fruits are beaked pods
Height: 1–3'

Shinyleaf spirea is a shrub found growing naturally in the northwestern states and Canada. It has been referred to commonly as white spirea or birchleaf spirea, as the leaves resemble those of birch trees. Another delightful common name that this plant has been given is "bridal wreath shrub," as the puffy white flower heads resemble a bouquet carried by brides. In the same genus, rose meadowsweet, *S. splendens*, grows at high altitudes in the park. Its short branches display charming flower heads that resemble rosy pom-poms.

AMERICAN DWARF MISTLETOE
Arceuthobium americanum
Sandalwood family (Santalaceae)
Quick ID: greenish-yellow whorled fanlike branches in trees; opposite, leathery scalelike leaves; small inconspicuous flowers
Height: 1.9–3.5"

Growing like small witches' brooms on the branches of infected trees, American dwarf mistletoe extracts water and nutrients from its host trees, robbing them of their needed food and water. Unlike most mistletoes that rely on birds to transport their sticky seeds, American dwarf mistletoes project their seeds outward from their lodgepole pine, *Pinus contorta*, hosts. In an event unknown in any other plant species, chemical changes heat up the seed cases, causing the tiny seeds to be dispersed in an exothermic reaction that propels the seeds outward at up to 24 feet per second. Flying up to 49 feet from the parent plant, the seed can infect surrounding trees, embedding their long threadlike roots into the branches of their powerless hosts.

ROCKY MOUNTAIN MAPLE
Acer glabrum
Maple family (Aceraceae)
Quick ID: lobed, toothed leaves; greenish-yellow flowers in clusters; smooth, gray bark
Height: 20–30'

Sometimes considered a small tree, the tall shrubby branches of Rocky Mountain maple never reach the size of maple trees found in the eastern states. This tall shrub produces paired fruits, called samaras, that are attached in a winged-shaped V. These tiny helicopters twirl downward from the branches, carrying the seeds away from the parent tree. American Indians used the strong, pliable wood for a variety of purposes including bows, arrows, snowshoes, fishing net hoops, and cradle frames. In fall, the leaves turn bright yellow, adding a splash of color to the fading season. The species name *glabrum* means "smooth," and *Acer* is the Latin name for all members of the maple genus.

SKUNKBUSH SUMAC
Rhus aromatica var. *trilobata*
Cashew family (Anacardiaceae)
Quick ID: yellow flowers on small spikes appear before the leaves; 3 alternate scalloped leaflets; fruit is a reddish berrylike drupe
Height: 2.6–4.6'

With a name like skunkbush, you may correctly suspect that this shrub does not have a pleasurable odor. To add to its dubious reputation, the 3-parted leaves highly resemble those of western poison ivy, *Toxicodendron rydbergii*. Skunkbush sumac leaves have a rather unpleasant skunk-like odor when crushed, but the buds and roots have actually been used as a deodorant. The sour but edible berries have been used to make a refreshing drink that resembles lemonade. American Indians mixed the berries with other foods for seasoning or dried them to make into jam. The bark and strong flexible stems were used to make baskets. The fruit is eaten by birds, bears, and other mammals, and the leaves are browsed by elk, pronghorn, and bighorn sheep.

WESTERN BLUE VIRGIN'S BOWER
Clematis occidentalis
Buttercup family (Ranunculaceae)
Quick ID: vine 1–11.5'; light purple 1.5–2" flowers with drooping heads; opposite leaves
have 3 leaflets that are somewhat heart-shaped and slightly serrated

Western blue virgin's bower is one of the few vines found in Yellowstone.
The delicate violet-blue flowers that gracefully hang downward are actually composed of sepals rather than petals. Sepals are modified leaves that
protect the flower parts. The Latin name *Clematis* comes from the Greek
clema, which means "vine," and *occidentalis* means "of the west." The
plant is sometime spelled "virginsbower." Blooming from May to July,
this plant grows best in shady, rocky areas and is sometimes called rock
clematis. After the flower blooms, the seeds form long plumes in a round
head and are dispersed by wind. The flowers of this vine were placed in
the hair of American Indian children to keep ghosts away.

HEARTLEAF ARNICA
Arnica cordifolia
Aster family (Asteraceae)
Quick ID: yellow daisy-like flower; opposite, heart- to arrow-shaped finely toothed leaves; single upright stem growing along a horizontal root (rhizome)
Height: 12–24" Bloom Season: June–August

As the name suggests, the lower heart-shaped leaves give this arnica its descriptive name. The bright yellow flowers resemble sunflowers, but if you look closely, the leaves of arnicas are positioned oppositely on the stem, while the leaves of most sunflowers are arranged alternately on the stem. Including varieties, 10 species of arnicas can be found in the park. Many mammals eat the plant, including mule deer, elk, and pronghorn; if they are not damaged, however, they can live up to 12 years. A tributary of Yellowstone Lake, Arnica Creek is named for these bright yellow flowers. Due to the heart-like shape of the leaves, this plant was used by American Indians in love potions.

196

ARROWLEAF BALSAMROOT ✓
Balsamorhiza sagittata
Aster family (Asteraceae)
Quick ID: bright orange-yellow daisy-like flowers; large 3.9–11.8" leaves covered with hairs especially on the undersides; bottom leaves triangular and pointed like an arrow; stem leaves smaller and oval
Height: 6–31"   Bloom Season: May–July

In late May and early June, the hillsides and meadows of Yellowstone burst into colorful palettes of bright yellow flowers that wave in the spring breezes. One of these tall yellow flowers is called arrowleaf balsamroot. Resembling small sunflowers, the arrowhead-shaped leaves surround clumps of flowers on solitary stems. Found mainly in the northern section of the park, arrowleaf balsamroot was widely used by American Indians medicinally and for food. The seeds were roasted and ground into a flour, the roots were cooked, and the stems and leaves were eaten like a salad. The roots were also used as incense during ceremonies. A similar yellow flower is mule ears, *Wyethia amplexicaulis*, but the leaves look like enormous mule's ears.

ELK THISTLE
Cirsium foliosum
Aster family (Asteraceae)
Quick ID: rosy-purple flower heads top tall stems; dissected, toothed leaves with spines
Height: 1–4' Bloom Season: June–August

Thistles are not known as anyone's favorite wildflower, but they do play a major role in the food web of insects, such as the multitude of bees that rely on their copious nectar. Several types of thistle can be found in the park, including Canada thistle, *C. arvense*, which is one of the nonnative, invasive species that can crowd out native plants. About 218 other invasive plants that are not historically found in Yellowstone have made their way into the park, including dalmation toadflax, *Linaria dalmatica*, ox-eye daisy, *Leucanthemum vulgare*, and spotted knapweed, *Centaurea maculosa*. Native thistles were said to be responsible for saving the life of Truman Everts, who was separated from his fellow travelers in 1870. By eating the edible roots, he was able to sustain his life until rescuers found him after 37 days.

WESTERN CONEFLOWER ✓
Rudbeckia occidentalis
Aster family (Asteraceae)
Quick ID: tall, coarse stem; 2" blackish-brown cylindrical cone; miniature yellow disk flowers; alternate egg-shaped pointed leaves that are slightly toothed
Height: 2–6'   Bloom Season: July–August

As a flower without any petals, western coneflower may be overlooked and viewed by some people as plain and unattractive, but this flower is recognized by plant ecologists as an important nectar plant for native bees, including the black-notched bumble bee, *Bombus bifarius*. Unlike most plants in the sunflower family, this one lacks the bright yellow ray-flower petals of most sunflowers. The dark-brown cylinder-shaped flower heads do have extremely tiny yellow ray flowers that smell a bit like chocolate-flavored cola. Native to the northwest, look for these unusual flowers between Norris and Mammoth Hot Springs.

TALL GROUNDSEL
Senecio serra var. *serra*
Aster family (Asteraceae)
Quick ID: 30–90 yellow flowers with 5–8 petals; shrubby stems; lance-shaped, finely toothed 3–6" leaves tapered at base
Height: 16–59" Bloom Season: June–September

Yellowstone's summers are filled with bright yellow daisy-like flowers that greet visitors to the park. One of these cheery yellow flowers is called tall groundsel, which is also known as butterweed groundsel and tall ragwort. Growing in tall shrubby clusters, the common name "ragwort" comes from the raggedy appearance of the flowers; *wort* is an Old English word for "plant." The word *groundsel* is also from the Old English and refers to a similar plant's use as a poultice for sores. Found in wetter areas, arrowleaf groundsel, *S. triangularis*, is very similar, but the leaves are blunt at the base, forming a long triangle. Although all are still in the aster family, some members of the genus *Senecio* have been moved to another genus, *Packera*, which better represents their characteristics.

WHITE MULE EARS ✓
Wyethia helianthoides
Aster family (Asteraceae)
Quick ID: 13–21 white petals on large daisy-like flowers; long, pointed, oval 7.8–15.7" leaves resemble a mule's ear
Height: 11.8–31" Bloom Season: May–July

Enticing visitors with the scent of vanilla, nutmeg, and citrus, white mule ears, or white wyethia, fills the breezes in Yellowstone. *Wyethia* is a group of wildflowers in the sunflower family.

The famous botanist Thomas Nuttall named this genus to honor Nathaniel J. Wyeth (1802–1856). Wyeth was a businessperson and explorer in the frontier west who sponsored an expedition that included Nuttall and John Kirk Townsend, another famous naturalist. Most species of *Wyethia* are yellow, but the petals of white mule ears are white, and the flowers remind you of a large daisy. Along with the yellow-flowered mule ears, *W. amplexicaulis*, both plants have pointed oval leaves over 12 inches long that resemble the ears of a mule, hence the common name.

COW PARSNIP ✓
Heracleum lanatum
Carrot family (Apiaceae)
Quick ID: large 4–8" flat clusters of small white flowers; maplelike leaves up to 12"; very tall, grooved hairy stem
Height: 3–10' Bloom Season: July–August

Growing up to 10 feet tall, this flat-topped white flower is found throughout most of the United States, except the Gulf coast and southernmost eastern states. With leaves up to 12 inches across, the genus name *Heracleum* appropriately honors Hercules, son of Zeus. Large mammals such as bear, elk, and moose eat the dinner-plate-size flowers and tender stems of this plant. The hairy foliage and stems can cause a sunburn-like rash. American Indians ate the peeled stalks either raw, like celery, or cooked. The roots were pounded and used to make poultices, which were applied to sores or bruises. The roots were also used to make a yellow dye. You can find cow parsnip still in bloom in August on the slopes of Mount Washburn.

FAIRY SLIPPER
Calypso bulbosa
Orchid family (Orchidaceae)
Quick ID: light pinkish-rose with purplish marks, yellow tuft of hairs on whitish lower petal; 1 oval leaf
Height: 2–9" Bloom Season: May–July

Orchids are among the favorite plants of many wildflower enthusiasts, and the gorgeous blooms of the fairy slipper or calypso orchid rival the most beautiful tropical orchids. This native showstopper is among over 15 species of orchids found in Yellowstone. The Latin name *Calypso* refers to the sea nymph of Homer's *Odyssey*, and *bulbosa* for the bulblike roots or corms. These delicate flowers grow in shaded forests. Bees soon learn that they have been tricked into visiting these dazzling flowers as they find that they do not provide any nectar reward, but hopefully pollination has occurred before the bee gives up. Remember that it is illegal to pick or damage any plant in the park.

TALL FRINGED BLUEBELLS
Mertensia ciliata
Borage family (Boraginaceae)
Quick ID: blue to pinkish nodding bell-shaped flowers; long arching stem; alternate, broadly lance-shaped leaves
Height: 1–3' Bloom Season: July–August

Dangling gracefully from arching stems, the nodding clusters of delicate bell-shaped blue flowers line shaded stream banks in the park. Also known as mountain bluebells or streamside bluebells, the flower buds are pink with blue tinges and turn blue as they open. In July, look for bluebells along LeHardy Rapids and in August at higher elevations such as Mount Washburn. Another very common and widespread blue bell-shaped flower is the harebell, *Campanula rotundifolia*, which has 1 inch upside-down tulip-shaped purple flowers. Harebells have oversized violet-blue flowers with fused petals that point sideways or slightly downward along spindly stems.

BITTERROOT
Lewisia rediviva
Purslane family (Montiaceae)
Quick ID: low growing; pink to white flowers up to 1" across with 12–19 petals; fleshy, tubular leaves that wither by the time the flower blooms
Height: 0.4–2"   Bloom Season: May–June

Always a treat but often a challenge to find, bitterroot grows in open, well-drained, rocky areas in the northern section of the park. The genus name, *Lewisia*, honors Meriwether Lewis (1774–1809), the famous American explorer who, along with William Clark, collected and documented many of the native plants growing in the unsettled western states. Since 1895, bitterroot has been the official state flower of Montana. American Indians cooked the bitter-tasting root that grew in the soil up to 12 inches deep, mixing it with berries or meat. The Bitterroot River and Mountains are named for this diminutive plant.

YELLOWSTONE SULFUR BUCKWHEAT
Eriogonum umbellatum var. *cladophorum*
Buckwheat family (Polygonaceae)
Quick ID: small, bright yellow flowers in bunch at top of stem; leaves and stem grayish and hairy
Height: 2–15.7" Bloom Season: June–August

Of the 41 species of sulfur buckwheats that are native to North America, about 10 different species or varieties are found in Yellowstone. Yellowstone sulfur buckwheat has a highly restricted range, only growing in the Upper, Midway, and Lower Geyser Basins to about Madison Junction. It is adapted to open, barren geothermal areas and is found growing in the Old Faithful area near the Visitor Education Center and Old Faithful Inn. The flowers are bright yellow in contrast to the pale yellow to whitish flowers of other species. A similar-looking flower with whitish flower heads is American bistort, *Polygonum bistortoides*. Bistort is common throughout the park in meadows and along roadsides.

PINEDROPS
Pterospora andromedea
Heath family (Ericaceae)
Quick ID: tall reddish-brown stem; pale-yellow urn-shaped flowers
Height: 1–4'   Bloom Season: July–August

Well camouflaged in conifer forests, the tall spires of pinedrops occasionally catch the eye of hikers along Yellowstone trails. Even though the plants can reach 4 feet tall, the reddish-brown stems blend well with the dappled forest light, making them difficult to see. Tiny yellow urn-shaped flowers hang down from the top of the stem that is covered with a sticky substance. The stem becomes woody when dry and often remains standing throughout the winter season. Pinedrops lack chlorophyll and are reliant on the roots of conifers and a soil fungus to provide nourishment. Look for pinedrops in wooded areas along the Upper and Lower Falls of the Grand Canyon of the Yellowstone.

ROCKY MOUNTAIN PHLOX
Phlox multiflora
Phlox family (Polemoniaceae)
Quick ID: low clumps; white flowers turning pink or violet, 5 petals, yellow center; small needlelike leaves
Height: 1.2–4.7" Bloom Season: May–July

Forming low mats of delicate white flowers, Rocky Mountain phlox is one of the species of phlox found in Yel-
lowstone. The fragrant flowers attract long-tongued pollinators such as moths, butterflies, and hummingbird moths. The word *phlox* comes from a Greek word that means "flame," as many species have bright, colorful petals. Hood's or spiny phlox, *P. hoodii*, also forms low mats, and the flowers are variable from white to bluish. Found in sagebrush areas of the park, the petals of longleaf phlox, *P. longifolia*, are variable but mostly pink-ish with upright stems. Cushion phlox, *P. pulvinata*, grows in subalpine and alpine habitats and forms cushion-like carpets.

BONNEVILLE SHOOTINGSTAR
Dodecatheon conjugens
Primrose family (Primulaceae)
Quick ID: magenta flower with 5 backward petals and yellow center; joined anthers point downward; basal, narrow, oval-shaped leaves; flexible stem with flower(s) at top
Height: 4–12"   Bloom Season: May–June

Bonneville or slimpod shootingstar is a distinctive wildflower native to northwest North America. Perched on a tall, thin leafless stem, shootingstars have strongly swept-backward, pink-magenta petals that imaginatively resemble shooting stars. The reddish stamens protrude from the flower like the tip of a missile. In about 8 percent of wildflowers, including shootingstars, bees shake the pollen from the anthers by vibrating their thoracic muscles in a unique process called buzz pollination. In May and June look for shooting stars in moist mountain meadows, including the pullout at Barronette Peak, where a pastel meadow of shootingstars and bluebells, *Mertensia* sp., follow fuzzy heads of pasqueflower, *Pulsatilla patens*.

LUPINE ✓
Lupinus sp.
Pea family (Fabaceae)
Quick ID: blue spikes of pealike flowers, 5–7 leaflets on fan-shaped leaf
Height: 4–35" Bloom Season: June–August

Lupines are a diverse group of wildflowers ranging from just several inches tall to shrub size. Most lupines (pronounced LOO pins) in Yellowstone are blue, but colors of lupines found in other areas vary greatly and include yellows, purples, reds, pinks, and whites. If you count the varieties of lupine species, there are 9 different lupines in the park, and most are notoriously challenging to identify. Silvery lupine, *L. argenteus*, alone has 5 varieties found in the park. Lupines sometimes form large colonies, and it was the mistaken thought that the plants robbed the soil of nutrients that lead to the name "lupine," which means "wolflike" or "ravenous." Lupines have root nodules containing nitrogen-fixing bacteria that allow the plant to deposit nitrogen, which actually replenishes the soil.

210

GREEN GENTIAN
Frasera speciosa
Gentian family (Gentianaceae)
Quick ID: tall stem; saucer-shaped flowers; 4 star-shaped greenish petals with bluish-purple spots and 2 fringed nectary glands at the base; leaves at the base of the plant are 10–20" long in a whorl around the stem
Height: 27.5–78.7"   Bloom Season: July–August

Green gentian is often called monument plant, as it is one of the tallest wild-flowers found growing in open meadows and fields. Often towering 4–5 feet above its neighbors, the unusual-looking plant has stunning 4-petaled greenish flowers with bluish-purple spots that attract a large number of pollinators. The leaves at the base of the plant are 10–20" long forming a whorl around the stem and becoming progressively smaller as they go up the robust stem. It grows for 20–80 years as a rosette of basal leaves before blooming. Like the century plant, *Agave americana*, of southwestern deserts, green gentian only flowers once during its life and then dies. Look for green gentian in the Canyon area and Mount Washburn.

211

ROCKY MOUNTAIN FRINGED GENTIAN
Gentianopsis thermalis
Gentian family (Gentianaceae)
Quick ID: deep blue to violet vase-shaped flowers; 4 overlapping 2" petals fringed on margins; inside center of the flower white often with purple stripes; leaves pointed or spatula-shaped
Height: 4–16"   Bloom Season: May–August

Rocky Mountain or meadow fringed gentian blooms gracefully in wet meadows and thermal areas of Yellowstone. A fair-weather friend, on cloudy days and when the sun has set, the petals twist closed, protecting the reproductive structures. The Latin name of this beauty, *Gentianopsis thermalis*, comes from the geothermal pools in Yellowstone where it is found. Based on different characteristics, gentians have been taxonomically split into three main groups. The fringed gentians that lack pleats between the petal lobes are now placed in the genus *Gentianopsis*, which means gentian-like. Similar blue to purple flowers include Idaho blue-eyed grass, *Sisyrinchium idahoense*, which has open star-shaped blue flowers, and harebell, *Campanula rotundifolia*, which has open tulip-shaped flowers that slightly nod or face horizontally.

STICKY PURPLE GERANIUM ✓
Geranium viscosissimum
Geranium family (Geraniaceae)
Quick ID: saucer-shaped flowers with 5 pinkish-purple petals; leaves in 5–7 coarsely toothed segments; leaves and stems with sticky glandular hairs; stems divided; fruits are capsules with hairs
Height: 1–2' Bloom Season: June–August

Blooming much of the summer, sticky purple geranium is a widespread flower in the western states. The 5 silky petals are lilac colored with deeper purple veins on the petals. This plant has sticky glands that can help protect the flower from insects. The leaves and roots of sticky geranium were used by American Indians as a cold remedy and as an eye treatment. It has also been used as an astringent to stop bleeding from cuts and wounds. The seeds are eaten by birds and mammals such as elk, and bears eat the leaves. Look for sticky geranium along open trails in the park.

213

ELEPHANTHEAD
Pedicularis groenlandica
Broomrape family (Orobanchaceae)
Quick ID: pinkish-purple irregular flowers on stalks; flowers resemble tiny elephant heads; fernlike divided leaves
Height: 1–2'   Bloom Season: July–August

Visitors to Yellowstone are often surprised when they take a close look at this amusing flower that is uniquely named elephanthead or elephantella. Upon close inspection, the tiny flowers sport 2 floppy petals that resemble "ears" and a long curved petal shaped like the upturned "trunk" of a little pink elephant, which is another common name for this flower. Growing in wet meadows, the purple spikes of small pink flowers can be seen in areas including along the trail to Observation Point near Old Faithful.

PAINTBRUSH ✓
Castilleja sp.
Broomrape family (Orobanchaceae)
Quick ID: variable colors; spikes of flowers; short leaves on spike
Height: 3.9–19.6" Bloom Season: June–September

Native to western North America, paintbrush flowers add bright splashes of scarlet flowers against a dark background of green leaves. The showy colored parts of paintbrushes are actually leaflike bracts and sepals. The actual flowers are hidden behind eye-catching colorful red bracts that serve to attract hummingbirds. The flower petals are fused into a narrow greenish-yellow tube. Paintbrushes are highly varied and come in a wide assortment of colors including red, pink, purple, yellow, and white. About 11 species have been recorded in Yellowstone. The red Wyoming paintbrush, *C. linariifolia*, was adopted as the state flower of Wyoming in 1917. The genus name, *Castilleja*, honors a Spanish botanist, Domingo Castillejo (1744–1793).

SEEP MONKEYFLOWER
Mimulus guttatus
Lopseed family (Phrymaceae)
Quick ID: 5 irregular yellow petals with 2 "lips" that have maroon dots; opposite leaves
rounded to heart shaped; grows in wet areas
Height: variable 0.6–2.3' Bloom Season: May–September

Monkeyflowers are so named for the 5 petals
that imaginatively resemble a monkey's face
with broad jaws. These intriguing and highly
variable flowers are always found growing in
wet areas, especially along streamsides. Seep
monkeyflower is also known as common or
yellow monkeyflower. American Indians
ate the slightly bitter leaves either raw or
cooked. It was used as an effective poultice
for wounds, rope burns, and cuts, as the
plant causes tissues to contract. Of the 8 species of monkeyflowers found in Yellowstone,
5 are yellow and 3 are pinkish-purple. Lewis'

monkeyflower, *M. lewisii*, is a showy pinkish-purple flower. Taxonomically, monkeyflowers are now placed in the lopseed family rather than the
figwort or snapdragon family.

PENSTEMON ✓

Penstemon sp.
Plantain family (Plantaginaceae)
Quick ID: 1" funnel-shaped flower with bottom "lips"; color varies from deep blue to
purple to pinkish; opposite leaves
Height: 2–27" Bloom Season: June–August

Over 275 species of penstemons grow as
beautiful wildflowers in a diversity of habitats
throughout North America. Eleven species
of penstemon can be found in Yellowstone,
and many of these are very similar, distin-
guishable only by subtle characteristics and
detailed measurements. These unique flowers are often called "beardtongue," as inside
the snapdragon-like flowers you can often see
tiny hairs on the protruding stamens. The
tubular or funnel-shaped flowers can range
from deep blue to purplish-pink. The wide
mouth is a perfect fit for large bees that enter

the flower for a nectar treat. Blooming in midsummer, look for penstemons throughout the park in dry meadows and rocky crannies.

217

GLACIER LILY
Erythronium grandiflorum
Lily family (Liliaceae)
Quick ID: pale yellow flowers; 6 nodding recurved petals (tepals); 2 lance-shaped leaves
Height: 3–11" Bloom Season: May–June

When the snow begins to melt, early spring visitors to Yellowstone are rewarded with scenes of bright yellow glacier lilies bounding skyward in the warming spring air. Glacier lily roots (slim bulbs or corms) were a staple for many American Indians in spring. Sometimes the roots were eaten raw, but more commonly they were cooked in soups or stews like small potatoes. Besides glacier lily, other plants were dug in spring to add to the soup pot, including spring beauty, *Claytonia lanceolata*. Grizzlies enjoy the sweet bulbs, too, and make quick work of the digging chore. As spring climbs up the tallest mountains, you can see glacier lilies blooming into June on Mount Washburn.

YELLOWBELLS
Fritillaria pudica
Lily family (Liliaceae)
Quick ID: narrow, yellow nodding bell-like flower; 2–4 narrow leaves
Height: 3.2–11.8"   Bloom Season: May–June

Often mistaken for glacier lilies, the small nodding flowers of yellowbells, or yellow fritillary, typically follow the emergence of glacier lilies. Yellowbells is a member of the genus *Fritillaria*, most of which are found only in western North America. *Fritillaria* comes from the Latin word *fritillus*, which means "checkered," and many of the species have these markings on the flowers. Yellowbells and glacier lilies are members of the lily family, and there are over 4,000 species worldwide, 7 of which can be found in Yellowstone. American Indians gathered the bulbs and cooked them for food.

LEWIS' FLAX
Linum lewisii var. *lewisii*
Flax family (Linaceae)
Quick ID: pale blue flowers with 5 petals and yellow center; several spindly erect stems; thin leaves; small, round fruit capsule
Height: 2–23.6" Bloom Season: June–August

A true early riser, the pale blue flowers of Lewis' flax open at sunrise but fall off by noon. The flat flowers offer bees and flies a handy landing platform for pollination. Also known as wild blue flax or prairie flax, the plants are eaten by elk, mule deer, and pronghorn. Even though Meriwether Lewis was not a trained botanist, his observations and collections of plants helped begin the discovery of the unique flora of the west. During the famed Lewis  and Clark Expedition, Lewis wrote about and described a species of flax that was not previously known to botanists. Later, during the cataloging and naming of plants from the expedition, Frederick Pursh honored Lewis when he named this wild blue flax *Linum lewisii*.

SAGEBRUSH VIOLET
Viola vallicola
Violet family (Violaceae)
Quick ID: 5 yellow petals with purplish lines on the lower 3 petals; rounded to oval leaves
Height: 1.2–5.9" Bloom Season: May–June

Sagebrush violet or yellow prairie violet grows in relatively moist areas characterized by sagebrush plains such as those in the northern section of the park. Violets such as sagebrush violet are yellow, but others in the park are white or blue. Of the 9 species of violets that can be found in Yellowstone, 3 are bluish, 2 are white, and the remaining 4 are yellow. All violets have 5 petals, with 2 at the top, 2 at the side, and 1 striped petal at the bottom. The lower petal acts as a landing pad for bees. The stripes, which are known as nectar guides, help direct the bee into the nectar source. Violet leaves are heart shaped, lance shaped, or finely divided.

FIREWEED
Chamerion angustifolium
Evening primrose family (Onagraceae)
Quick ID: spires of rose-pink flowers with 4 petals; alternate, narrow leaves; reddish stems
Height: 2–6' Bloom Season: July–August

Aptly named, fireweed is one of the first plants to grow after a forest fire or other soil disturbance. The magenta flowers are often a striking contrast to the blackened soil and trees. Fireweed spreads from underground stems, and the small seeds that are encased in erect, slim pods are attached to fluffy, white hairs, which ensures  wide dispersal. Elk enjoy the plant as food, and hummingbirds and butterflies sip the nectar. Thanks to recent botanical and genetic research, the genus was taxonomically changed from *Epilobium* to *Chamerion*; therefore, older plant books may refer to that genus.

YELLOW POND LILY
Nuphar polysepala
Water lily family (Nymphaeaceae)
Quick ID: aquatic; large, floating, heart-shaped 4–16" leaves; yellow, cup-shaped, 3–5" flower
Height: 1–3"   Bloom Season: July–August

Over 10 percent of the plants in Yellowstone are ones that depend on the lush water-filled ponds, lakes, and wetlands in the park. In July, the water-loving yellow pond lilies begin blooming atop large, floating heart-shaped leaves. The flowers and leaves are on separate stems, but both are attached to long, submerged roots called rhizomes. Yellow pond lily was an important source of food and medicine for American Indians. The roots soothed the pains of rheumatism, and a root concentrate was used as a sore-throat gargle. The edible seeds pop like popcorn, and they were dried and ground into flower or cooked and eaten. Other wetland plants in the park include broadleaf cattails, *Typha latifolia*, with its noticeable brown flower spikes and tall leaves.

YELLOW COLUMBINE
Aquilegia flavescens
Buttercup family (Ranunculaceae)
Quick ID: pale yellow to pinkish-yellow, nodding flowers with 5 petals with a long slender spur; light yellow spreading sepals behind the petals; spindly stalk; wedge-shaped leaves divided into 3s
Height: 8–27" Bloom Season: June–August

Yellow columbine is a graceful light yellow flower. The nodding flower has 5 pale backward-pointing spur-like petals with pale yellow borders. The tips of the pointed spurs contain nectar. Probing for the sweet treat, humming-birds inadvertently pollinate the flower. The genus name *Aquilegia* comes from the Latin word *aquila*, which refers to an eagle's talons. The common name *columbine* is derived from the Latin word *columba*, which means "dove," and if viewed closely and with a little imagination, the long necks and heads of 5 doves taking flight rings true. Look for yellow columbine in moist areas throughout the park, including the trail to Mount Washburn.

LITTLE LARKSPUR

Delphinium bicolor

Buttercup family (Ranunculaceae)

Quick ID: 1–15 dark purplish-blue flowers with whitish centers; flowers have long spur on the back

Height: 4–16"   Bloom Season: June–July

Larkspurs add rich color to the lush green meadows of Yellowstone. Up to 15 beautiful, deep purple flowers are arranged near the top of an irregular greenish stem. American Indians used the flower to dye quills and arrows. Women made an infusion with the plant to shine and straighten their hair. In the park, little larkspur and upland larkspur, *D. nuttallianum*, grow in similar habitats and are often difficult to distinguish. Mountain larkspur, *D. glaucum*, has 25 or more pale blue to lavender flowers and is very tall. Burk larkspur, *D. burkei*, or tall meadow larkspur, has linear leaves. In the same family, the very similar Columbian monkshood, *Aconitum columbianum* (inset), resembles larkspur, but the upper part of the flower looks like a hood on a cape.

FOXTAIL BARLEY
Hordeum jubatum
Grass family (Poaceae)
Quick ID: greenish-purple stems; long 1–3" green bristles (awns) fade to white
Height: 1–2'

Foxtail barley is a very noticeable grass in many areas of the park. Native to the western United States, it has spread into most of the country. Though beautiful, the seed heads have sharp, pointed joints that can stick in the nose and mouth of grazing animals including deer, elk, and pronghorn. Resulting infections can cause lumpy abscesses and can result in death.

ARROWGRASS
Triglochin sp.
Arrowgrass family (Juncaginaceae)
Quick ID: erect stems; small green flowers develop into brown fruits; grasslike leaves
Height: 3.9–27.5"

Resembling tall arrows, the stems of arrowgrass are visible in meadows just north of Madison and near Old Faithful. These plants are not really grasses but in their own family. Containing hydrogen cyanide, the plants are toxic, and, if ingested, death can result from respiratory failure.

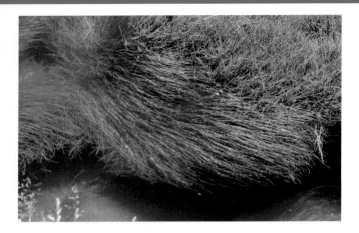

WARM SPRING SPIKERUSH
Eleocharis flavescens var. *thermalis*
Sedge family (Cyperaceae)
Quick ID: dark green; lies flat in water; reddish-brown top
Height: to 16"

One of the most eye-catching plants in Yellowstone is a plain green wetland plant called warm spring spikerush or pale spikerush. A member of the sedge family, warm spring spikerush typically grows in warmer climates; it can't stand cold water. Here in the park, however, it finds the thermal runoff waters ideal and flourishes even in the harsh winters. You can see warm spring spikerush growing along Obsidian Creek about 1 mile south of Roaring Mountain. A few plants, such as Ross' bentgrass, *Agrostis rossiae*, and Tweedy's rush, *Juncus tweedyi*, also thrive in the thermal areas where other plants can't take the heat.

SMOOTH SCOURING RUSH
Equisetum laevigatum
Horsetail family (Equisetaceae)
Quick ID: jointed stem with whorls of tiny scalelike leaves, spores in cone-like structure at tip of stem
Height: 12–31"

Resembling tall asparagus plants, scouring rushes or horsetails are ancient wetland plants, some of which grew to tree-size proportions during the Carboniferous period (about 300 million years ago). Six species are found in Yellowstone, including smooth scouring rush. The common name "horsetail" and the Latin name *Equisetum* come from the resemblance of some branched scouring rushes, like field horsetail, *E. arvensis*, to a horse's tail.

LEATHERY GRAPE FERN
Sceptridium multifidum
Adder's tongue family (Ophioglossaceae)
Quick ID: leathery dissected triangular leaves, tiny green grapelike spores on separate 6–17.7" stalk
Height: 3–12"

Leathery grape fern is an unusual looking but inconspicuous plant that grows in meadows in Yellowstone National Park. New fronds appear late in the year, during July through September, and the spore-bearing stalk is evident. As new genetic information arises, many plants, including leathery grape fern, have undergone a Latin name change. The old genus, *Botrychium*, has recently been change by taxonomists to *Sceptridium* for this and other grape ferns.

FRAGILE FERN
Cystopteris fragilis
Cliff fern family
(Woodsiaceae)
Quick ID: clustered fronds, broad lance shaped fronds, stalks reddish at base
Height: 4–12"

Fragile fern is well named as the brittle fronds break easily when bent. This small fern is found on moist, protected areas where it can get a toehold, including cracks in rocks, such as those found on Soda Butte hot spring cone in Lamar Valley. Ferns reproduce by spores that are encased under the bottom of the frond in protective dots called sori. When the sorus dries, it opens, releasing the spores to be carried off in the wind.

WESTERN BRACKEN
Pteridium aquilinum var.
pubescens
Bracken fern family
(Dennstaedtiaceae)
Quick ID: large, long arching stem, leaves at end divided into 3 triangular parts
Height: 2–6'

Western bracken fern is on individual upright stems rather than clusters and forms large colonies. Although the tender fronds of bracken have been traditionally cooked and eaten in spring, it is now known to contain carcinogens and should be avoided as a food source.

DRY ROCK MOSS
Grimmia sp.
Grimmia moss family (Grimmiaceae)
Quick ID: dark-green to blackish cushions or tufts on rock; white hairs on leaf tips create a grizzled appearance

Like all mosses, dry rock moss does not have roots or flowers. Mosses are very simple plants that absorb water and nutrients mainly though their leaves, like a sponge. When mosses reproduce, they send up tiny stalks called sporophytes with spores growing inside. Similar to the seeds of many flowering plants, spores travel through the air by wind to form new plants. Most mosses require moist environments, but dry rock moss is specialized to be able to survive in harsh, dry conditions and can colonize exposed, bare rock habitat. Much of the year, it looks gray and dead, but it turns green again after a rain. Found worldwide, dry rock moss is one of 325 species in this family.

UMBRELLA LIVERWORT
Marchantia polymorpha
Marchantia family (Marchantiaceae)
Quick ID: leathery; often liver-shaped 1" segments that come together; grows flat on moist soil

Liverworts are primitive plants that lack vascular tissue, such as xylem and phloem that carry water and nutrients in trees. Instead of roots, liverworts anchor to the soil with simple appendages called rhizoids. Liverworts have the capability of reproducing both sexually and asexually, giving these plants a greater chance of survival. The resemblance of liverworts to a liver caused people to believe that they could be used to cure diseases of the liver. Umbrella liverwort or common liverwort produces antifungal and antibacterial properties and is currently undergoing studies as a potential drug for medicinal use. Umbrella liverwort is an early colonizer of burned areas, and mats of liverworts help prevent soil erosion until other plants can revitalize the area.

TREE-HAIR LICHEN
Bryoria fremontii
Shield lichen family (Parmeliaceae)
Quick ID: dark brown; hangs from trees in thick, twisted hairlike strands with thinner perpendicular side strands
Type: fruticose (shrubby)

Tree-hair lichen, or wila (wee-la), grows in long, dense, hairlike strands on conifers. It has long been used as food, typically by baking it into a lichen cake in a fire pit. American Indians used it as a tonic and to treat indigestion and diarrhea. It was also used as absorbent fiber for diapers and lining moccasins. Tree-hair lichen is also an important source of food and nesting material for the northern flying squirrel, *Glaucomys sabrinus*. According to legend, this lichen came about when coyote's hair became entangled in a tree. After cutting himself loose, he vowed that his hair should never go to waste, and hence it became food for people to eat.

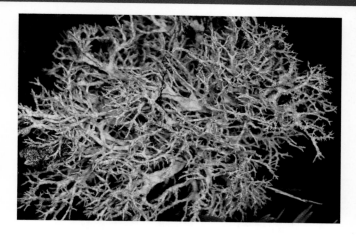

WOLF LICHEN
Letharia vulpine
Shield lichen family (Parmeliaceae)
Quick ID: bright greenish-yellow; thin branching strands
Type: fruticose (shrubby)

Poisonous beauties of the forest, long, bright greenish-yellow strands of wolf lichen hang gracefully from conifer trunks and branches. This lichen contains the yellow pigment vulpinic acid, which was used as an important source of yellow dye. Vulpinic acid acts as a repellent for some herbivores. It shows some activity against gram-positive bacteria. Wolf lichen was once used in Europe to poison wolves and foxes, generating its common name.

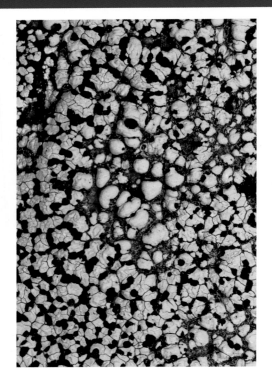

YELLOW MAP LICHEN
Rhizocarpon geographicum
Map lichen family (Rhizocarpaceae)
Quick ID: Yellow tiles, black dots interspersed
Type: crustose (flat)

Pieced together like a stone walkway, the yellow map lichen grows very slowly. At a growth rate of about 0.44 inches per century, map lichens are used to determine the age of geologic events such as a glacial retreat. This use of lichens to determine relative age of exposed rock is called lichenometry. The idea is that the largest lichen is the oldest, and if the growth rate is known, the minimum age of the rock can be determined.

WOOLY FOAM LICHEN
Stereocaulon tomentosum
Snow lichen family (Stereocaulaceae)
Quick ID: pale greenish-gray; forms mounds; finely divided crinkled tips
Type: fruticose (shrubby)

This conspicuous and beautiful lichen can be found in the Grant Village area. It grows on the ground in wooded areas along with mosses and mushrooms. The stalks look rigid but are soft and pliable. This family of lichens is called the snow lichen family, as they look like they have been dusted with snow. Members of this family were often used to make orange and brown dyes.

BLISTERED ROCK TRIPE
Umbilicaria hyperborea
Umbilicate family (Umbilicariaceae)
Quick ID: dark lavalike surface with drops of small, wrinkled, gummy drops; attached to rocks
Type: foliose (leafy)

A lichen is actually 2 organisms that grow together as 1 living entity. In a mutualistic relationship, a fungus provides shelter, and an algae photosynthesizes the sun's energy. Sharing resources, they can live in areas where neither could grow alone. Lichens absorb dust and other particulate matter from the air, which is how they obtain nutrients. This also makes them very sensitive to whatever is carried in the air, and lichens are well known indicators of air pollution. Along with yellow map lichen, *Rhizocarpon geographicum*, and elegant sunburst lichen, *Xanthoria elegans*, blistered rock tripe is one of the first lichens to recolonize burned areas.

BLUSHING ROCK TRIPE
Umbilicaria virginis
Umbilicate family (Umbilicariaceae)
Quick ID: dark gray to brownish-gray; wrinkled surface with crystal-like particles in center and scattered black tar-like spots; lower surface pale buff or pink; attached to rocks
Type: foliose (leafy)

The rock tripes are often considered survival food, but those who have tried them have likened the taste and texture to tough cardboard. Rock tripe or naval lichen grows from a central "stalk" that is attached to the surface of a rock. The edges are brittle when dry but leathery when wet. American Indians added it to soups as a thickening agent. Lichens may represent many of the oldest life forms on Earth, with some recorded as over 4,500 years old. Lichens are considered a very important stage in the succession of soil making. Look for blushing rock tripe at high elevations, including the Mount Washburn area.

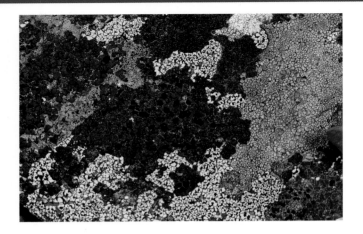

TILE LICHEN
Various sp.
Disk and tile lichen family (Lecideaceae)
Quick ID: grows flat on the surface (usually on rocks)
Type: crustose (flat)

There are several types of lichens that look like they were fit together like tiny kitchen tiles, which are appropriately called tile lichens. Particular lichens grow on particular types of rocks, and tile lichens are usually found on acidic rocks such as the volcanic and metamorphic rocks in the park. Lichens appear in many forms and colors, growing on rocks, trees, and soil. The flat crustose lichens, such as tile lichens, grow on rocks so tightly they cannot easily be peeled off. Leafy lichens are called foliose; others have bushy structures and are called fruticose. Some that are flattened and attached to the substrate in the middle are called umbilicate.

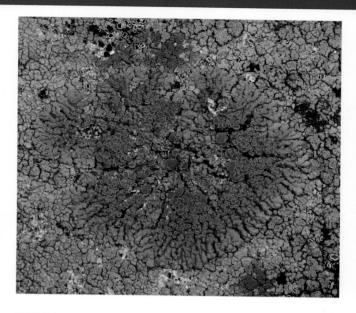

ELEGANT SUNBURST LICHEN
Xanthoria elegans
Sunburst lichen family (Teloschistaceae)
Quick ID: bright orange patches on rock
Type: crustose (flat)

Colorful sunburst lichens often grow near the vicinity of pika, marmots, or bird roosts, as they grow best in nutrient-rich environments that are well fertilized. Found on all continents except Australia, the elegant sunburst lichen has a widespread alpine distribution. It has high amounts of carotenoids, which are pigments that enhance the photosynthetic properties as well as protect the plant from the damaging effect of ultraviolet (UV) light. These pigments are responsible for the orange coloration of this lichen. In medical trials, the sunburst lichen helped break down certain agents that cause cancer.

FLY AGARIC
Amanita muscaria
Amanita family (Amanitaceae)
Quick ID: large; reddish-orange cap with white spots; white stalk

This legendary mushroom is the mystical fungus of fairy tales and stories told throughout the world. In some cultures, fly agaric has religious significance and has been identified in mythological tales due to its biologically active agents. Toxic doses may be found in as little as 1 cap. Some members of the amanita family of mushrooms contain some of the most poisonous substances known to science. Seven species of amanitas have been found in the park.

WEBCAP
Cortinarius sp.
Cortinarius family
(Cortinariaceae)
Quick ID: brown; often slimy cap; gills
rusty-brown

Over 100 species of Cortinarius have been identified in Yellowstone; over 2,000 species of this very large genus have been identified worldwide. A silky veil or cobweb-like fibers that protect the gills of the mushroom identify members of the genus *Cortinarius*. As the mushroom ages, this veil breaks apart, leaving behind remnants in strings. This silky veil is called a cortina, which means "curtained." One way that mycologists identify mushrooms is by their spore color, and all Cortinarius mushrooms have a rusty-brown spore print.

BISON DUNG FUNGI
Psilocybe merdaria
Hymenogaster family (Hymenogastraceae)
Quick ID: small, light yellowish-brown; grows in dung

Found growing in nutrient-rich patches of bison dung, *Psilocybe merdaria* are small, yellowish-brown, nondescript mushrooms. Fungi in the genus *Psilocybe* often contain the psychoactive compound psilocybin and are sometimes referred to as "magic mushrooms." Psilocybin has properties associated with serotonin, but ingestion can lead to toxic reactions. Bison dung fungi is nonpsychoactive, but it plays a major role in decomposing the copious amounts of dung deposited by the large animals in the park.

SCULPTURED PUFFBALL
Calbovista subsculpta
Lycoperdon family (Lycoperdaceae)
Quick ID: white to brown; softball size; feltlike, warty surface; sterile base

In the whimsical world of fungi, mushrooms can take many shapes and forms. Puffballs are round fungi that can grow to basketball size or can be as small as a marble. Young puffballs are white and firm inside at first, but as they mature the spore mass inside turns yellowish, then brown and powdery. When forces such as wind, rain, or an animal open the mature puffballs, the spores spill out and are spread in the wind. The giant western puffball, *Calvatia booniana*, is very similar to the sculptured puffball and is also found in the park.

YELLOW TRICOLOMA
Tricholoma equestre
Tricholoma family
(Tricholomataceae)
Quick ID: yellow to orangey cap; whitish-
yellow thick stem; yellow gills

This mushroom goes by several common names, including yellow knight, saddle-shaped tricholoma, and man-on-horseback. About 10 species of *Tricholoma* mushrooms have been identified in Yellowstone. Many of these mushrooms are very similar and require microscopic identification of spores. Mushrooms range from delicious edibles to those that are deadly poisonous. Some species of *Tricholoma* were commonly eaten, but cases of poisoning have been reported. Never eat a wild mushroom unless it has been identified by an expert.

KING BOLETE
Boletus edulis
Bolete family (Boletaceae)
Quick ID: 2.5–8" cap; color varies from
yellowish to reddish-brown; thick stalk

Boletes have pores rather than gills under the cap where the fungal spores reside. King bolete is a favorite edible mushroom that is often sautéed in butter or dried and used in soups, gravies, or as a flavoring. It grows commonly in coniferous forests where it forms a mutualistic, symbiotic tree-root relationship called an ectomycorrhizal association, supplying the tree with needed nutrients and water. Both organisms benefit in the relationship as the tree supplies needed carbohydrates for the fungus.

BLUE STAIN SLIPPERY JACK

Suillus tomentosus
Suillus family (Suillaceae)
Quick ID: bolete; spongelike pores that stain blue when bruised; yellowish-tan cap and stem

Blue stain slippery jack is a type of bolete mushroom that has spongy pores under the cap rather than straight gills. This fungus grows symbiotically with lodgepole pines and aids the trees with nitrogen-fixing bacteria that it hosts. Its edibility is questionable, as it can cause diarrhea and vomiting. Another mushroom in this genus, *S. sibiricus*, is only found growing symbiotically with whitebark pine at high altitudes in the park.

ROUNDED EARTHSTAR
Geastrum saccatum
Earthstar family (Geastraceae)
Quick ID: leathery or papery; brown to tan to whitish; triangular rays surrounding a globe with hole in top

The first time you see an earthstar, it may remind you of a child's old toy lying on the ground. Earthstars are a type of puffball mushroom that hold the spores in the center. The triangular-shaped rays help stabilize the mushroom to keep it from turning over in the wind. It's fun to touch an earthstar and watch the cloud of dark smoke (spores) puff out of the top of the mushroom.

TRAIN WRECKER
Neolentinus lepideus
Brown rot family (Gloeophyllaceae)
Quick ID: flat to convex brown cap; ring on stem (stipe)

Fungi are neither plants nor animals. They are classified into their own kingdom, Fungi, which is shared by molds, mildews, and other microscopic fungi that produce disorders including athlete's foot. Yellowstone harbors some unique fungi that thrive at high temperatures in geyser areas. These thermophilic (heat-loving) fungi assist plants that grow in the geyser areas and allow them to exist. Many fungi play a vital role in the ecosystem as important decomposers, breaking down the dead matter into usable elements. Members of the brown rot family of mushrooms are specialized in decaying wood. These mushrooms can decompose railroad ties, leading to the common name of this mushroom—"train wrecker."

BLACK MOREL
Morchella sextelata
Morel family (Morchellaceae)
Quick ID: brownish-black conical honeycomb or vertical netlike ridges; hollow stem

Black morels are one of the 4 species of morel that are adapted to wild-fire areas. These species come in after a fire, but their numbers decline with each passing year. Delicious to eat, grizzly bears have been known to dine on these delicacies. Many wild animals depend on mushrooms as a source of food. Please don't pick or destroy any plant or fungus in the park.

ORANGE LATEX MILK CAP
Lactarius deliciosus var. *areolatus*
Russula family (Russulaceae)
Quick ID: bronzy-orange to dull yellow; cap slightly depressed in center; yellowish gills
that ooze orangey latex when cut, then turns green

When damaged or cut, all members of the genus *Lactarius* ooze milky latex, but in this species the latex is bright orange. The part of the mushroom that we see is only the reproductive part of the fungus. The living body of the fungus is hidden from view, usually underground or in wood. Smaller than human hairs, tiny filaments branch and grow into

a mass called the mycelium, which is the body of the fungus. When conditions are right, the mycelium yield spore-producing, fruiting bodies that emerge as mushrooms.

ROSY RUSSULA
Russula sanguinea
Russula family (Russulaceae)
Quick ID: cap and stalk pinkish-red; dull
white gills

The bright red caps of russulas make them easy to spot on the green for-est floor. Of the 200-plus species documented in North America, over 15 species of russulas have been identified so far in Yellowstone. The various species of russulas are sometimes quite similar and often provide expert mycologists with identification challenges. The gills of many rus-sulas are brittle and, when they fall off, they look like almond flakes.

SPINY ROSE GALL WASP
Diplolepis bicolor
Gall wasp family (Cynipidae)
Quick ID: round with many pinkish spines

You may notice unusual round, spiky balls on the stems of wild roses that look like the weapons of small gnomes. These odd-looking growths are not caused by supernatural beings; instead the culprits are non-stinging wasps called cynipid wasps. Cynipid wasps are small, black, and shiny with a narrow waist. The female injects her eggs into the plant, causing a defensive reaction by the plant's tissues. The plant's goal is to isolate and encase the intruder to keep it from spreading throughout and damaging the entire plant. The wasp larvae grow inside the gall and eventually chew their way out and begin feeding on the plant leaves. About 40 species of wasps cause galls on roses.

SAGEBRUSH WOOLY BUD GALL
Rhopalomyia medusirrasa
Gall midge family (Cecidomyiidae)
Quick ID: round; green with some brown; tufts of hairs

Many species of insects, including gall midges, fruit flies, and a mite, rely on sagebrush as host for their young. The plants serve as a shelter and source of food for the developing larvae. Over 28 species of small flies called midges specifically depend on big sagebrush, *Artemisia* sp. In turn, there are some insects such as weevils that specialize in eating galls that have been induced by other insects, which often kills the young larvae growing inside the gall. Other insects, including grasshoppers and beetles, prey on the gall insects. Birds and other wildlife prey on the larger insects as well as the gall insects. The sagebrush habitat, thus, supports a vital microcosm of life.

SPONGE GALL MIDGE
Rhopalomyia pomum
Gall midge family (Cecidomyiidae)
Quick ID: round or lobed; large, up to 1.7" in diameter; soft spongy; green to reddish-brown

These large rounded galls are one of the most commonly seen galls on big sagebrush, *Artemisia tridentata*. These galls begin to develop in late fall, and the midge larvae grow inside until spring, when they emerge as adults in May to June. After mating, the females deposit their eggs on the sagebrush buds, and the cycle repeats. Most of the galls contain either male or female midges, with only a few producing both males and females. Harvester ants, *Pogonomyrmex owyheeli*, lie in wait to prey upon the emerging adults. Other insects, such as wasps, make use of these large galls to raise their young, too.

WILLOW APPLE GALL
Pontania sp.
Common sawfly family (Tenthredinidae)
Quick ID: small, round red berrylike ball on leaf

Willows are susceptible to gall growth, and many species of insects, including midges, sawflies, and mites, cause willow galls. Willow gall sawflies are small wasps that have sawlike ovipositors that they use to deposit their eggs into the leaf tissue. The plant responds by forming a reddish berrylike growth on the leaf. The larva grows here, nourished by the plant tissue, until they leave the gall. Several different insects and birds feed on the larva within the galls.

BASALT

Quick ID: dark blackish or gray (weathers into rusty-red)

Type: igneous rock

Curious vertical columns of basalt, formed from solidified lava that looks like giant hexagonal stone fence posts, can be seen near Tower Fall in Yellowstone National Park. The rapid cooling of a thick flow of lava creates cracks and fractures that shape the lava into columns of rock. Basaltic columns can also be seen at Sheepeater Cliff.

OBSIDIAN
Quick ID: glassy dark black
Type: igneous rock

Obsidian is formed when lava that contains lots of silica cools and crystallizes very quickly as it erupts. Nine miles north of Norris Junction you can see Obsidian Cliff along the road. American Indians made use of the strength and fracturing properties of obsidian by forming knives, spear points, and projectile points. When obsidian is formed, the original geophysical circumstances are unique, and the location of its origin can be traced by geologists; 10,000 years ago, obsidian artifacts from Yellowstone were traded by prehistoric people in what is now Ohio.

PETRIFIED WOOD

Quick ID: generally dark brown or black with a wooden form

Type: sedimentary rock

Near Tower-Roosevelt, the Petrified Tree display reminds you of the volcanic activity that has shaped the park. Trees must be buried very quickly with lava from volcanic eruptions to prevent decay; silica in the groundwater then soaks into the tree and eventually hardens, preserving the wood. The petrified tree that we can see here was uncovered by erosion. Remember that collection of any fossils, rocks, or any other materials is illegal in the park.

TRAVERTINE
Quick ID: white, often with bands of tan, cream, rusty colors
Type: sedimentary rock

Calcium carbonate deposits resulting from hot springs form the sedimentary rock known as travertine. A form of limestone, travertine is deposited by minerals from hot springs, such as those at Mammoth Hot Springs. Geothermal activity supplies the heat necessary to warm the water that seeps down through thick layers of sedimentary limestone formed from ancient seas. The travertine terraces at Mammoth Hot Springs change rapidly from variations in water flow and temperature. The remains of trees engulfed by travertine are evidence of the constantly changing activity.

References

Arora, D. *Mushrooms Demystified*. 2nd ed. Berkeley, CA: Ten Speed Press, 1986.

Brinkley, E. S. *Field Guide to Birds of North America*. New York: Sterling Publishing Co., 2008.

Brodo, I. M., S. D. Sharnoff, and S. Sharnoff. *Lichens of North America*. New Haven, CT: Yale University Press, 2001.

Bryan, T. S. *The Geysers of Yellowstone*. 3rd ed. Boulder: University Press of Colorado, 2001.

Chapple, J. *Yellowstone Treasures: The Traveler's Companion to the National Park*. 4th ed. Oakland, CA: Granite Peak Publications, 2013.

Cobb, B. *A Field Guide to Ferns and Their Related Families*. New York: Houghton Mifflin, 1984.

Craighead, F. C., Jr. *A Naturalist's Guide to Grand Teton and Yellowstone National Parks*. Guilford, CT: FalconGuides, 2006.

Craighead, J. J., F. C. Craighead, and R. J. Davis. *A Field Guide to Rocky Mountain Wildflowers*. Boston: Houghton Mifflin, 1963.

Craighead, K. *Large Mammals of Yellowstone and Grand Teton National Parks*. Yellowstone National Park, WY: Yellowstone Association, 2006.

Cripps, C. L., and L. Eddington. "What Do We Know about Fungi in Yellowstone National Park?" *Yellowstone Science* 20, no. 1 (2012): 8–16.

Davis, R. M., R. Sommer, and J. A. Menge. *Field Guide to Mushrooms of Western North America*. Berkeley: University of California Press, 2012.

Dunkle, S. W. *Dragonflies through Binoculars: A Field Guide to Dragonflies of North America*. New York: Oxford University Press, 2000.

Eversman, S. "Lichens in Yellowstone National Park." *Yellowstone Science* 15, no. 3 (2007): 14–19.

Forsyth, A. *Mammals of North America: Temperate and Arctic Regions*. Buffalo, NY: Firefly Books, 2006.

Fritz, W. J., and R. C. Thomas. *Roadside Geology of Yellowstone Country*. 2nd ed. Missoula, MT: Mountain Press Publishing Company, 2011.

Gruson, E. S. *Words for Birds: A Lexicon of North American Birds with Biographical Notes*. New York: Quadrangle Books, 1972.

Halfpenny, J. C. *Yellowstone Wolves in the Wild*. Helena, MT: Riverbend Publishing, 2003.

Harris, A. G., E. Tuttle, and S. D. Tuttle. *Geology of National Parks.* 6th ed. Dubuque, IA: Kendall/Hunt Publishing, 2004.

Harris, M. *Botanica North America.* New York: HarperCollins, 2003.

Hart, J. *Montana Native Plants & Early Peoples.* Helena: Montana Historical Society and Montana Bicentennial Administration, 1976.

Hendrix, M. S. *Geology Underfoot in Yellowstone Country.* Missoula, MT: Mountain Press Publishing, 2011.

Janetski, J. C. *Indians in Yellowstone National Park.* Salt Lake City: University of Utah Press, 2002.

Kershaw, L. J., A. MacKinnon, and J. Pohar. *Plants of the Rocky Mountains.* Edmonton, AB, Canada: Lone Pine Publishing, 1998.

Kiver, E. P., and D. V. Harris. *Geology of U.S. Parklands.* 5th ed. New York: John Wiley & Sons, 1991.

Lamplugh, R. *In the Temple of Wolves.* Published by author, 2014.

Leftridge, A. *The Best of Yellowstone National Park.* Helena, MT: Farcountry Press, 2014.

Lesica, P. *Manual of Montana Vascular Plants.* Fort Worth, TX: BRIT Press, 2012.

Little, E. L. *National Audubon Society Field Guide to North American Trees, Western Region.* New York: Alfred A. Knopf / Chanticleer Press, 1980.

Marschall, M. C., and J. S. Marschall. *Yellowstone Trails: A Hiking Guide.* Yellowstone National Park, WY: Yellowstone Association, 2013.

Mathews, C., and C. Molinero. *The Yellowstone Fly-Fishing Guide.* Guilford, CT: Lyons Press, 1997.

Mathews, D. *Rocky Mountain Natural History, Grand Teton to Jasper.* Portland, OR: Raven Editions, 2003.

McEneaney, T. *Birds of Yellowstone.* Boulder, CO: Roberts Rinehart, 1988.

Milne, L., and M. Milne. *The Audubon Society Field Guide to North American Insects and Spiders.* New York: Chanticleer Press, 1980.

Moerman, D. E. *Native American Ethnobotany.* Portland, OR: Timber Press, 1998.

Moerman, D. E. *Native American Food Plants.* Portland, OR: Timber Press, Inc., 2010.

Montana State University. *Living Colors: Microbes of Yellowstone National Park.* Yellowstone National Park, WY: Yellowstone Association, 2013.

References

Page, L.M., and B. M. Burr. *Peterson Field Guide to Freshwater Fishes of North America North of Mexico.* 2nd ed. New York: Houghton Mifflin Harcourt, 2011.

Parks, R. *Fishing Yellowstone National Park.* 3rd ed. Guilford, CT: Lyons Press, 2007.

Petrides, G. A. *A Field Guide to Trees and Shrubs.* 2nd ed. New York: Houghton Mifflin, 1986.

Phillips, H. W. *Central Rocky Mountain Wildflowers.* 2nd ed. Guilford, CT: FalconGuides, 2012.

Poole, S. *Butterflies of Grand Teton & Yellowstone National Park.* Moose, WY: Grand Teton Association, 2009.

Russo, R. *Field Guide to Plant Galls of California and Other Western States.* Berkeley: University of California Press, 2006.

Schiemann, D. A. *Wildflowers of Montana.* Missoula, MT: Mountain Press Publishing, 2005.

Schneider, B. *Best Easy Day Hikes Yellowstone National Park.* 3rd ed. Guilford, CT: FalconGuides, 2011.

Schneider, B. *Hiking Yellowstone National Park.* 3rd ed. Guilford, CT: FalconGuides, 2012.

Shaw, R. J. *Plants of Yellowstone and Grand Teton National Parks.* Camano Island, WA: Wheelwright Publishing, 2000.

Sheehan, K. B., D. J. Patterson, B. L. Dicks, and J. M. Henson. *Seen and Unseen: Discovering the Microbes of Yellowstone.* Guilford, CT: FalconGuides, 2005.

Sibley, D. A. *The Sibley Guide to Birds.* 2nd ed. New York: Alfred A. Knopf, 2014.

Streubel, D. *Small Mammals of the Yellowstone Ecosystem.* Boulder, CO: Roberts Rinehart, 1989.

Streubel, D. *Small Mammals of Yellowstone and Grand Teton National Parks.* Pocatello, ID: Windy Ridge Publishing, 2002.

Taylor, R. J. *Northwest Weeds.* Missoula, MT: Mountain Press Publishing, 2011.

Tilt, W. *Flora of Montana's Gallatin Region.* Bozeman, MT: Gallatin Valley Land Trust, 2011.

Vitt, D. H., J. E. Marsh, and R. B. Bovey. *Mosses, Lichens & Ferns of Northwest North America.* Vancouver, BC, Canada: Lone Pine, 1988.

Vizgirdas, R. S. *A Guide to Plants of Yellowstone & Grand Teton National Parks.* Salt Lake City: University of Utah Press, 2007.

Wells, D. *100 Birds and How They Got Their Names*. Chapel Hill, NC: Algonquin Books of Chapel Hill, 2002.

Whitacre, J. O. *National Audubon Society Field Guide to North American Mammals*. New York: Chanticleer Press, Inc., 1996.

Wilkinson, T. *Watching Yellowstone & Grand Teton Wildlife*. Helena, MT: Riverbend Publishing, 2004.

Wilson, D. E., and S. Ruff, eds. *The Smithsonian Book of North American Mammals*. Washington, DC: Smithsonian Institution, 1999.

Yellowstone National Park. *Yellowstone Resources and Issues Handbook: 2014*. Yellowstone National Park, WY: Yellowstone National Park, 2014.

Glossary

accipiter: hawk with short, rounded wings and relatively long tail.

achene: dry, one-seeded fruit with the outer wall enclosing the seed.

alkaloid: bitter compound produced by plants to discourage predators.

alternate leaf: growing singly on a stem without an opposite leaf.

anther: tip of a flower's stamen that produces pollen grains.

arboreal: living in trees.

archaea: single-celled microorganisms that lack a nucleus.

basal: at the base.

bulb: underground structure made up of layered, fleshy scales.

buteo: raptor with broad wings and relatively short tail.

cache: storage area of food.

caldera: remnant of a collapsed volcano, creating a usually circular crater.

capsule: a dry fruit that releases seeds through splits or holes.

carrion: remains of deceased animal.

catkin: a spike, either upright or drooping, of tiny flowers.

commensalism: a type of symbiosis where one species benefits while a second species is neither harmed nor benefitted.

compound leaf: a leaf that is divided into two or more leaflets.

corm: rounded, solid underground stem.

deciduous: a tree that seasonally loses its leaves.

diurnal: active by day.

drupe: outer fleshy fruit usually having a single hard pit that encloses a seed.

ecosystem: a biological environment consisting of all the living organisms in a particular area, as well as the nonliving components such as water, soil, air, and sunlight.

ectomycorrhiza: a mutualistic, symbiotic relationship between a fungus and the roots of plants. The fungus supplies nutrients and water for the plant, and the plant supplies carbohydrates for the fungus.

endemic: growing only in a specific region or habitat.

entomology: the study of insects.

ethnobotany: the study of the relationship between plants and people.

evergreen: a tree that keeps its leaves (often needles) year-round.

fumarole: steam vent from superheated water.

genus: taxonomic rank below family and above species, always capitalized and italicized.

geyser: hot springs with constrictions that prevent water from circulating freely, therefore causing an eruption under pressure.

glean: pick small insects from foliage.

habitat: the area or environment where an organism lives or occurs.

harrier: slender hawk with long wings and rounded face.

host: an organism that harbors another organism.

hot spring: superheated water caused by underground magma.

hydrothermal: water heated by underlying molten rock.

introduced: a species living outside its native range; often introduced by human activity.

leaflet: a part of a compound leaf; may resemble an entire leaf but it is borne on a vein of a leaf rather than the stem. Leaflets are referred to as pinnae; the compound leaves are pinnate (featherlike).

local resident: nonmigratory species found year-round in an area; also "resident."

metamorphic life cycle: change of structure during an animal's life stages.

metamorphic rock: a rock that has been altered by extreme heat and pressure, such as gneiss, schist, or quartzite.

midden: a pile or mound of deposited food or refuse.

migrate: movement of birds between breeding grounds and wintering areas.

mud pot: acidic features with limited water supply; the escape of various gasses through wet mud causes bubbling.

mutualism: a type of symbiosis where both organisms benefit.

mycology: the study of fungi.

Glossary

mycorrhiza (pl. mycorrhizae): the symbiotic, mutually beneficial relationship between a fungus and the roots of a plant.

nape: area at the back of the neck.

native: a species indigenous or endemic to an area.

nectar: sweet liquid produced by flowers to attract pollinators.

niche: an organism's response to available resources and competitors (like a human's job).

nocturnal: active at night.

omnivore: animal that feeds on a variety of foods, including both plant and animal materials.

opposite leaves: growing in pairs along the stem.

parasitism: one organism benefits at the expense of another organism.

pollen: small powdery particles that contain the plant's male sex cells.

pollination: transfer of pollen from an anther (male) to a stigma (female).

polygynous: the breeding system of males having more than one mate.

poultice: soft, moist mass, typically made of plants, applied to wounds or to heal sickness.

raptor: birds of prey that hunt and feed on other animals.

rhizome: underground stem that grows horizontally and sends up shoots.

sepal: usually green, leaflike structures found underneath the flower.

snag: dead tree that remains standing.

species: taxonomic rank below genus; always italicized but never capitalized, also called "specific epithet."

stamen: male part of the flower composed of a filament, or stalk, and anther, the sac at the tip of the filament that produces pollen.

supervolcano: a volcano capable of an eruption of more than 240 cubic miles of magma.

symbiosis: association of unlike organisms that benefits one or both.

taxonomy: study of scientific classifications.

thermal feature: a geological feature heated by underlying molten rock.

thermophile: an organism that lives in hot environments.

toothed: jagged or serrated edge.

torpor: short-term state of decreased physiological activity, including reduced body temperature and metabolic rate.

travertine: a deposition of calcium carbonate.

wing bar: line of contrasting colored plumage formed by the tips of the flight feathers of birds.

winged: thin, flattened expansion on the sides of a plant part.

Index

Index

Index

About the Authors

Professional photographers, biologists, authors, and noted national park experts, Ann and Rob Simpson have spent years involved with research and interpretation in US national parks. They have written numerous books on national parks coast to coast that promote wise and proper use of natural habitats and environmental stewardship. As a former chief of interpretation and national park board member, Rob has a unique understanding of the inner workings of the national park system. In cooperation with American Park Network, both have led Canon "Photography in the Parks" workshops in major national parks, including Yosemite, Yellowstone, Grand Canyon, and Great Smoky Mountains.

Ann and Rob are both award-winning biology professors at Lord Fairfax Community College in Middletown, Virginia. With a background in science education, Ann heads the science department. As part of the college's nature photography curriculum, the Simpsons regularly lead international photo tours to parks and natural history destinations around the world.

Long known for their stunning images of the natural world, their work has been widely published in magazines such as *National Geographic*, *Time*, *National Wildlife*, and *Ranger Rick*, as well as many calendars, postcards, and books. You can see their work at Simpson's Nature Photography: agpix.com/snphotos.